DAD IN A CHEER BOW

Patrick Riccards

Author's Tranquility Press
ATLANTA, GEORGIA

Copyright © 2023 by Patrick Riccards

All rights reserved. No part of this publication may be reproduced, distributed or transmitted in any form or by any means, including photocopying, recording, or other electronic or mechanical methods, without the prior written permission of the publisher, except in the case of brief quotations embodied in critical reviews and certain other noncommercial uses permitted by copyright law. For permission requests, write to the publisher, addressed "Attention: Permissions Coordinator," at the address below.

Patrick Riccards/Author's Tranquility Press
3800 Camp Creek Pkwy SW Bldg. 1400-116 #1255
Atlanta, GA 30331, USA
www.authorstranquilitypress.com

Ordering Information:
Quantity sales. Special discounts are available on quantity purchases by corporations, associations, and others. For details, contact the "Special Sales Department" at the address above.

Dad in a Cheer Bow/Patrick Riccards
Paperback: 978-1-962859-02-8
eBook: 978-1-962492-74-4

Dedication

To Anna,

I will always have the pleasure of being your father and now have had the honor of being a coach to you and your friends. I thought you were kidding when you first asked if I would be a cheer coach. It is an experience that I will always cherish, and it is because we were able to do it together. Thank you for allowing me to share this incredible journey with you. You will always be my favorite flyer!

Acknowledgments

First, I would like to thank my daughter Anna, who has made this entire journey possible. When you came to me as a third grader, asking me to coach your competition cheer squad, I didn't quite understand where that request would lead. Because of you, I have become a better father and a better man. I'm proud to be your father and your coach.

Additionally, thanks must go to Christine Olenchalk. I will never know what you thought when a precocious young girl asked you if her dad could join your coaching staff. When you welcomed me to your team, I tried to give you a gracious way out. Each day since, I'm glad that you didn't accept. It has been an honor to be your assistant coach for the past four seasons. Through the highs and the lows, I have enjoyed each and every moment of it. You accepted me into the cheer coach sorority from day one.

To Minda Alena, who I shared the mat with for four consecutive seasons as assistant coach. You have been my cheer wife all these years. I couldn't think of a better partner for this crazy journey.

To Robin Resnick and Reenuada Howard, my fellow assistant coaches who have been there with me for the highs of Globals and Nationals, and the lows of cheering during Covid. You will always be my sisters. As will Amber Spataro, who was always there as a coach in arms over the years.

To all of my Wildcat cheer daughters, who saw that I could be both a dad and a cheer coach well before I ever figured it out. Each season, I returned to the sidelines because of you. Each year, I sought to do better by you, to help make you better athletes and stronger young women. I just hope I have lived up to your expectations. You have exceeded mine.

To all of our cheer moms (particularly Evelyn, Jennifer, Jennifer, Joei, Marianna, Stephanie, and Tisha), who have trusted me with their daughters and supported having a "boy" cheer coach on the mat. Know I will always be there to cheer on your daughters.

And special thanks to my wife, Jennifer, the strongest, loudest cheerleader in my life who has supported me through this journey and accepted all of the uncertainty, anxiety, and self-doubt that came from my years as a cheer coach. You were amused by the idea of me coaching from the beginning, without knowing exactly how much of my time and attention cheer would take. You accepted all that cheer has taken from me (and you) over the years, and all that I have taken from it. Without your support and help, I never would have been able to be the sort of coach I wanted to be.

And to the cheer coach at Eastern Regionals who once told me that men had no business coaching competition cheer, how do you like me now?

CONTENTS

Section 1 The Inaugural Season
- Chapter 1 How It All Started 6
- Chapter 2 Becoming an Assistant Coach 17
- Chapter 3 Facing my Fears 24
- Chapter 4 The Sleepover 38
- Chapter 5 Setting up the Base 45
- Chapter 6 The First Competition 54
- Chapter 7 Showmanship 63
- Chapter 8 Jersey Wild 71

Section 2 Succeeding in Adversity
- Chapter 9 Losing a Quarter of the Squad 82
- Chapter 10 Disney Dream Crushed 87
- Chapter 11 YCADA Globals 91
- Chapter 12 Better Coach for My Cheer Daughters 98

Section 3 Achieving the Disney Dream
- Chapter 13 Pushing Harder 104
- Chapter 14 Getting Ready for Central Jersey 109
- Chapter 15 Competition Time 113
- Chapter 16 Eastern Regionals 117
- Chapter 17 Getting to Florida 121
- Chapter 18 Showtime 125
- Chapter 19 Results 130

Section 4 Cheering in the "New Normal"
   Chapter 20   A New Year and COVID-19 136

Section 5 Life Lessons
   Chapter 21   Manning Up for Cheer 144
   Chapter 22   The Luckiest Man of Earth 154

About the Author

From 2017 through 2020, Patrick Riccards served on the coaching staff for the West Windsor-Plainsboro, New Jersey Wildcats Cheer team, working with WWP's Junior Pee Wee, Pee Wee, and Junior Varsity squads. His PW squad took second place at YCADA Globals and his JV squad earned a top 10 finish at Pop Warner Nationals. Patrick is the founder and CEO of the Driving Force Institute for Public Engagement and its award-winning Untold History initiative.

Pat is the author of the Indie Book Award-winning *Dadprovement: A Journey from Careerist to Adoptive Father to a Real Husband and Dad* and the lead editor and contributing author of *Why Kids Still Can't Read: Continuing to Challenge the Status Quo in Education*. He also writes and engages on social media as Eduflack. Pat lives in Florence, South Carolina with his wife, Jennifer, and children, Michael and Anna.

Preface

"You're a boy cheer coach?" In the era of "girl dads," my story is a one that fascinates a lot of people. Divided into four sections, this book describes a journey filled with fun, struggles, commitment, and excitement of being a cheer coach for my tween (and now teen) daughter's competition cheerleading team.

This book is a memoir detailing my experiences coaching my daughter and her cheer squad. Coming with absolutely no understanding about cheer or cheer competition, after working so closely with a deeply committed team of girls and coaches, cheer soon became part of my DNA. I love all of these cheerleaders as if they were my own daughters and have learned a ton from them.

A collection of memories, experiences, and the stories that I can tell, this is an attempt to get it all down on paper while reflecting on some of the significant lessons that I learned throughout this journey. Cheer has been a great part of my life, and I have no doubt that the past four years will always remain close to my heart as a treasured memory.

Section 1

The Inaugural Season

Chapter 1

How It All Started

"All our dreams can come true, if we have the courage to pursue them."

— Walt Disney

My daughter, Anna, usually has a sparkle in her eyes and a spring in her step. She is an active girl with a mind of her own who is always wanting to indulge in something new. Children's interests are fickle and ever-changing. For instance, a child could begin to invest her time in ballet only to realize that she's actually more interested in joining the school choir or the baseball team. Some are very ambitious and take up many activities simultaneously only to give them up one by one as they quickly lose interest. It is not until a child sticks to a certain sport or activity with consistency that they are able to master it. Anna was no different.

Anna is a bright girl, and at age 7 she was exceptionally energetic. However, her energy needed to be channeled, and as parents, we realized that we had to help her find an activity that she would consistently enjoy participating in. Parents often find themselves living vicariously through their children; that was not the case with my wife, Jennifer, and me. We encouraged our children to try whatever they showed interest in, and supported them until they decided they were done with that activity, but felt strongly that we shouldn't push them to do things they didn't want to try or continue. They had to fulfill their commitment, but they didn't need to make it a life-long one.

Life offered many opportunities for us to experience something new. In 2014 we moved from Connecticut to New Jersey. Before we moved, Anna was heavily into horseback riding. We would go to the stables every week where this tiny little girl insisted on saddling the largest of the available animals. For competitions, they would put her on smaller, more manageable steeds, which would just make her angry and frustrated.

On one occasion, when Anna was saddled on the largest horse at the stables, she was bucked and thrown off her saddle. Physically, she was fine, but that was the end of horseback riding for her. One has to fail if one wants to excel at something, failure teaches a person how to succeed. But for young Anna, that fall was just one time too many.

As parents, we realized early on that she doesn't like losing. I gave her a pep talk on the importance of learning to accept failure with grace. She questioned if I, too, had failed in life, and I told her that every person has to face their fears and failures; without that, we would never move forward. While she did seem to understand the point of the conversation I had with her, horseback riding was still off the table, she was too scared to continue.

Just the way horseback riding was a short-lived hobby for Anna, she dabbled in various activities such as Tae Kwon Do and soccer. She was like most girls her age. As much as she liked to follow the trend and take up activities that her friends participated in, we found that her interest would soon dwindle.

Even if she possessed the aptitude, as Anna did for soccer, she was bored easily. Furthermore, she disliked being told what to do, which, unfortunately for her, is a key part of being on a sports field. Her frustration at being directed by a coach or instructor only led to increased disinterest.

It was fascinating for us as parents to see Anna shift from one sport to another, but we wished she would be consistent with something so that we could see her excel in that area. She has a lot of natural physical talent, as well as an ability to work hard when she wants to, and we wanted to see her shine.

The shift from Connecticut to New Jersey also marked a shift in Anna's interests. With the end of horseback riding, we had to find a new activity to keep her involved in, and so we asked her what interested her the most. Her immediate answer was, surprisingly, "cheerleading."

Unfortunately, our moving schedule didn't quite work with cheer in our new community. We relocated in late summer, and didn't realize until September that cheer practice began at the beginning of August, which meant we had missed the window for that year. Anna took the news well and focused on the start of school. Later during second grade, she took an interest in mixed martial arts, a sport that she pursued for years. But she never forgot about her interest in cheer.

She reminded us of this during the summer before the start of third grade, and this time around, we were aware of the admission dates and signed her up for the 'Mighty Mites' cheer squad. We saw her and her seven- and eight-year-old friends cheer on the sidelines for a team of similarly-aged Mighty Mite football players throughout the fall. They learned basic motions. They learned basic stunts. They even memorized a handful of cheers to perform each game.

This cheerleading wasn't exactly ESPN level, but it was definitely fun to watch. What surprised my wife and me was the seriousness with which Anna devoted herself to it. She seemed to have finally found that one activity that gave her inner satisfaction. Anna never skipped practice and made it a point to be at every single game. At the start of the season, she attempted not to let the summer sun get to her. She begged to have her new dog come to each game to watch her.

She was also willing to put in the extra work as her cheer team prepared for a regional competition. That fall, being so young, her squad wasn't competing to score the highest number of points or to advance on the next round of competition. Instead, it was to simply perform in an arena and give the team a sense of what competition was like. And it was a great learning experience for Anna. Kids often get drained because of the rigorous training that is required to excel, but this time we were proud to see Anna stick around long enough to get past the elementary level.

With the end of the first cheer season, we returned the uniform and got back to our regular routines. Christmas holiday, spring, and the end of the school year kept us so occupied that cheer was amongst the last things on our minds. My wife and I were under the impression that cheer was like many of the other sports our daughter had played in previous years. We assumed that by the end of the year, she would have had enough of cheerleading, and it would be time to move on to something new.

Boy, were we wrong! When the summer before fourth grade started, it turned out that Anna had been talking to other girls from her squad and was determined to cheer again. One of her good friends decided to stay with the younger, less intense,

Mighty Mite squad for another year so she could have time to pursue other interests like theater. Anna, on the other hand, decided it was time to move up to be a member of the Junior Pee Wee squad, with all the expectations and harder work that would be required.

I guess I should admit here that at that point, I knew little about cheer. Back in high school, I had many friends who were cheerleaders, and it was heartening to see the effort that they put into it, but truth be told, I had no clue about the sport. The little knowledge that I had of cheerleading stemmed from movies such as 'Bring It On,' so I knew enough to crack some jokes about spirit fingers. Jen was even less aware than I was. Her high school didn't have cheerleaders and she had a very preconceived – and not so positive – notion of what a cheerleader was.

Irrespective of what my wife or I thought about cheerleading, the fact of the matter remained that Anna wanted to pursue it. And so, we respected her choice, especially since she felt so strongly about it. As parents, we felt it was our job to support our daughter in whatever she wanted to achieve. But knowing that both of our children had a tendency to get zealously involved in something only to get bored of it within a short time span, we gave Anna a peptalk about cheer being a responsibility. Signing up for Junior Pee Wee meant that she was making a commitment to her coaches and her squad; she would have to see it through until the end of the season, even if she got bored or wanted to do other things.

It would mean that she would scale back the mixed martial arts practice where she was taking four or five kickboxing and grappling classes a week. Anna happily used this as an opportunity to hit pause on grappling – similar to high school wrestling – a part of the training she wasn't keen on anyway.

When we signed Anna up for cheer, we were in for a surprise. We had no idea of what the time commitment was that required, even for an eight-year-old. Anna was expected to attend practice for two hours every night on weekdays for the entire month of August, or about eight to ten hours a week under the hot New Jersey August sun. She was required to condition, drill, and practice with her squad. Anna was mentally prepared to give her best, and she remained committed. She would gather her towel, water bottle, and cheer bucket and troop off to the park, often without even complaining.

As one of the smaller girls on the squad and as one of the most flexible members, it was quickly determined that Anna would be a 'flyer.' That meant she would be one of the cheerleaders who would be lifted up and thrown around during her routines. Anna couldn't have been happier about the designation. As her parents, we weren't quite so enthusiastic!

Just like most seasons, that first season of Junior Pee Wee began with quite a bang. A group of nine- to eleven-year-old girls all tried to learn what they needed to learn, demonstrate what they needed to demonstrate, and then come together as a team in short order. With school starting and football games happening on Sunday afternoons, practices shifted to Tuesday and Thursday evenings. Then, as the squad got closer to the regional competition, Saturday afternoon practices began. For Anna and another of the squad's flyers, a special tumbling class was added on Wednesday evenings. Surprisingly to us, Anna was all in.

The level of her commitment not only surprised me but genuinely inspired me. Even as a parent, I always tried to learn from my children, and by being motivated and steadfast in her mission, Anna had taught me the value of being devoted to a cause.

One thing to know though is that despite showing such commitment, Anna was bored with one key aspect of cheerleading. Performing at the Junior Pee Wee football games was particularly frustrating for Anna as they did the same cheers each week. There wasn't much stunting or tumbling involved. To her, it was fairly rote. Her lackluster attitude was apparent every week.

However, her focus on the upcoming cheer competition was unwavering. All of the girls knew that they needed to win two cheer competitions to make it to Nationals at Disney World. The squad would need to take one of the first two spots at the first competition to advance to the second. Then they'd need to again come in the top two to head on to the Happiest Place on Earth.

The goal of this team was to get to Disney, and they worked extremely hard for it. Every practice session would end with a cheer of determination focused on achieving this goal. With the first competition approaching in October, the team was starting to gel. The results of all the practices could be seen clearly. The routines were getting tighter and crisper. The girls were learning to trust each other. If all went as planned, this was going to have a happy ending.

It didn't take long for us to figure out that we had a family scheduling glitch. When the date and time of the first competition were announced, we discovered that it was on the same weekend as Jennifer's stepsister's wedding. The family was supposed to be up in the Berkshires, not at the Sun Arena in Trenton.

We had to make a decision that worked out for everyone, and what made the most sense was for Jennifer and our son, Michael, to pack up their party clothes and attend the big wedding in Massachusetts while Anna and I stayed behind to prepare for cheer.

While we wished that the whole family could attend the wedding, we were very clear that our children came first, wherever possible. Cheerleading was not just a casual hobby for Anna. It was something she was pursuing with great seriousness, and thus we were going to do everything we could to help her succeed.

The fact that Anna and I share a very unique father-daughter bond helped get us through this time. When Anna was five years old, she decided that she wanted to go for regular pedicures, and not just that, she wanted me to accompany her. So every month, I would find myself seated in a spa chair next to my daughter, getting my nails painted a color of Anna's choice. I've never seen another man in one of those chairs, but that didn't matter to me; all that I cared about was my daughter's happiness. As some say, it's the smallest of things that take up the most space in our hearts; the moments you spend with your child today become memories for them to cherish forever.

For years, Anna and I did kickboxing together. My wife and son also eventually took up the sport, but Anna would proudly tell everyone that she had been at it longer than both of them. We do a lot of things together, including clothes shopping, to the extent that I was the one who accompanied her when, at the age of eight, she wanted to buy sports bras for daily wear. With such a healthy relationship, my staying home to be the designated "cheer mom" for the weekend was no big thing to us.

But a few of the girls on the squad and their moms likely found it strange when I was the only father to turn up with his daughter at the "curling party." This was a team bonding ritual the night before every competition, as the girls' hair was prepared for the next day's competition. When I was at a loss as to what to do, thankfully one of the junior coaches offered to take care of Anna's hair. So, all that was required of me was to hang out with the moms and then bring Anna home with her head full of those old-style foam curlers.

My appearance at practices and games had become an accepted occurrence, and everyone was aware of Jen's absence due to the family wedding. As we waited in the arena the next day at the competition, the moms and I all discussed ways to calm the anxious girls' nerves. They just wanted to do their best, and we needed to give them morale boosters, telling them that they were indeed the best and would make it to the top. We all anxiously discussed whether we would move on to the next round, and I joked that we should sell liquor in the stands to relieve the nerves of the parents at the next competition. Even though other dads were not present, I felt relaxed and accepted in my Wildcats Cheer t-shirt while rooting for my squad.

The girls secured second place that day, but it didn't matter to them whether they had come in first or second; what did matter was that they were moving on to the next competition. They then had a few weeks to improve their game and achieve their dream of going to Disney.

Ambition is a fiery friend that keeps you going till the end, and these girls were the most ambitious girls I had ever met. Their desire to make it to Disney was so strong that it helped them overcome all the obstacles that they faced.

As the frequency of practices increased, so did the girls' level of seriousness. The coaches added stunts that might help them score an extra point or two. Anna was asked to do more tumbling than she had in the first competition, and she took it in stride.

Coincidentally, the regional competition saw us need to split up as a family again, because that Saturday was my grandmother's 99th birthday party. Right after the girls competed, our son and I would head north to the event, while Jen and Anna would stay behind to see how they scored. The day started extra early as I got Anna to the arena by 7 am to ensure we were all ready for business.

Once the girls had trooped off to wait in the wings with their coaches, I joined the other cheer moms in setting up our Wildcats section. At the first competiton, we realized that we hadn't done a good enough job of decorating our cheering section, so this time we went all out in our decorating. We wanted to be loud and supportive when the girls came out, so some of the moms had also brought beads and noisemakers.

As we were finishing up the decorating, one of the cheer moms showed me an orange tutu (the team's colors were orange, black, and white) that she had picked up at the party store. I told her it looked terrific and was just perfect for her. She shook her head and said, no, she had gotten it for me.

Not wanting to be a spoilsport, I agreed to put it on. There I was, in a sea of cheer moms, wearing my Wildcats Cheer t-shirt, a pair of tiger ears, and a fluffy orange tutu. Cheering on our squad. Screaming myself hoarse. I then spent the rest of the morning walking around the arena in my getup, which included stopping to take pictures with the entire squad (and even some random parents on other teams!) I immediately became an official mascot.

Unfortunately, the season ended with the squad coming in third place; we were not meant to go to Disney that year. At that point, Anna declared that she was done with cheer. She didn't want to do it again. To be honest, Jen and I were a little relieved. Cheer took up a lot of time in the fall for all of us. We could now look forward to a little flexibility.

We wanted to make sure that Anna didn't want to continue cheerleading, so as the school year continued, we would ask her about it from time to time. Anna insisted that she was done with Wildcats. Her coach wanted her back, given that most of the squad was returning and they had high hopes for Nationals the next year. Anna would occasionally pause to reconsider, but would always say no.

Then in the spring, she decided to go to a party with her old squad. Initially, Anna just wanted to see her friends again. But as they were talking about cheer, she started thinking about it some more. Part of her wanted to do it again. Part of her was afraid of being a flyer again and having someone drop her (it had happened at games the previous season, but not during competition). Part of her wasn't sure.

Jen and Anna came home from the cheer party with some interesting news. Anna had talked to her coach. She had agreed to return to the cheerleading squad for another year. With one condition. Her dad had to be an assistant cheer coach. Rah, rah, rah!

Chapter 2

Becoming an Assistant Coach

"Life's not a spectator sport. If watchin' is all you're gonna do, then you're gonna watch your life go by without you."

— Laverne, 'The Hunchback of Notre Dame'

Anna's track record of moving on from one sport to another made it seem highly unlikely to us that she would ever be consistent and committed to any one activity. We really wanted to see her excel at something and discover her niche but that only would happen if she decided to stick it out. After Anna's indecision about doing cheer another year at the end of the last season, I was pretty surprised when she answered, "If I do it again, can Daddy be my coach?"

In all honesty, I felt I was in quite a tricky spot because I knew absolutely nothing about cheer. During Anna's first season, I served as team photographer and was enthused to see her and the other Mighty Mites out there on the field. The next year, Anna was a flyer, and I held my breath watching her lifted high in the air for every game and every competition. The little bit of knowledge that I had pertaining to the sport stemmed from watching movies and from remembering cheer friends in high school. However, I was incapable of naming the motions and couldn't tell whether they were being done correctly or incorrectly.

So when she asked if I would coach, I did what any father would do. I said, "Sure." I wanted my daughter to be happy. And I figured she would completely forget about the question before she had to ultimately decide on rejoining the cheer squad many months later. I never imagined I would have to live up to my promise.

As a father, I feel it is incumbent upon me to devote myself to the happiness of my children, no matter what it takes. And a request to become a cheer coach seemed like a very small thing to me. It would be exhausting and time consuming, to say the least, but it would be equally fulfilling because it would mean that I would see the twinkle in my daughter's eyes every time she introduced me to her friends as her coach (or at least I hoped to see that twinkle!) It seemed to be something that mattered to Anna immensely, and that in itself held great weight with me. I couldn't let my daughter down.

Given that I had expected the matter to be soon forgotten, I was quite taken aback when Anna and Jen came home and informed me that evening that I indeed was going to be a cheer coach. It became a reality a month or so later when I received an email from the head coach, welcoming coaches back to the squad and noting that I was joining as a new assistant.

I immediately responded to her email, thanking the coach for including me. And I duly informed her that I really knew nothing about cheer and would be perfectly content if she didn't want to use me or if she just needed me to carry things between practices for the squad. Instead, I was told the more help, the better, and was given web links for the mandatory Youth Cheer and Dance Association (YCADA) coach training and CDC concussion training I'd have to complete before I could join the squad. For a moment, I thought about how, if I flunked the courses, I couldn't fulfill my coaching duties. But my responsibility to my daughter was too strong. I managed to complete both courses on my first try, and I have the certificates of completion to show for it.

All that meant I was ready to go for the start of summer "training camp," that period where the entire squad would go through two-hour-a-day practices four nights a week, Monday through Thursday. The goal was to spend the month of August helping the returning cheerleaders remember all they learned the previous season while introducing a handful of new girls to the squad. This is where we would start to evaluate what each girl was able to bring to the team and what role each could play.

Meeting one of the other assistant coaches for the first time on the first night, I remarked to her that I was scared to death of being out here on the football field. And I wasn't kidding. We had a squad of 17 girls, with a head coach, three assistants, and three junior coaches (high school students) – all female. We had parents on the sidelines watching the football practice, mostly mothers. The closest I came to having another male on the field (except for the football coaches) was a small dog who was there with one of the moms watching.

As we did team introductions, I was Coach Pat. I'm not sure if it was more awkward for me to be in the circle with all the girls or for them to have a "boy" coach there with them. Anna was immediately embarrassed as we went around and introduced ourselves (names, grades, favorite ice cream, etc.), and I noted I was "Anna's dad." She didn't think I needed to say that because everyone knew.Fortunately, it was the only time during training camp that I did embarrass her, or at least that she admitted to.

Being a hands-on parent and indulging your children's whims not only benefits your children by making them feel that you care, but is also good for us as parents and individuals. For me at least, I was able to gain a new sense of energy by being actively involved with the girls. The moments I spent on the field with my daughter and her squad certainly rejuvenated me and made me feel closer to my daughter at the same time.

However, I felt I really had to take care of a few things in my new role as cheer coach. When cheer practice started, I was very conscious about breaking the common stereotype about men, that we love talking about ourselves and just didn't listen. I agree that many men do tend to dominate conversations, particularly in new situations. And we are known for not listening, but, as far as I was concerned, I knew nothing, so I wanted to listen and learn as much as I could and as quickly as I could.

So I was quiet. When with the other coaches, I'd only speak if I was asked a question. I smiled a lot. I tried not to talk about myself or try to bring conversations back to my experiences. It was a new and eye-opening experience for me.

Another one of my conscious decisions was to refrain from asking the girls to do anything that I myself wouldn't do. Being a coach, I felt I had to model the right behavior and set the right tone for our practice sessions. So from day one, I was on the grass, doing strength training with them. Burpees. Walk forwards. Push-ups. Lunges. I did the stretches as well, though poorly, trying to get down into a split as low as my fireplug body would allow. But I was trying. And I hoped the girls could see that.

It also meant that I would do the cheer motions with the girls. Trying to remember what I learned in my online course, and doing my best to watch the junior coaches, there I was showing the girls what a clean, a high V, a T, etc., looked like.

Fortunately, I had remembered most of the words from the cheers from watching Anna the previous season. It was one of the few pluses I had going for me in those early days. It was hard enough to learn the motions as we did it, but at least I knew what to say!

Initially, I felt a bit out of place amids all the women, but soon I grew used to it, and it took about a week for everyone to get used to having me around too. It wasn't as strange for all of us. However, my greatest fear was realized when our junior coaches were all off at the beach, and the other two assistants happened to be away from practice as well. So everything depended on just me and the head coach. She began to run the girls through a routine and quickly realized that, while most of the girls knew it, we had four or five for whom it was entirely new.

So as Coach Chris took those few off to the side to teach them the routine, she turns and says, "Coach Pat, why don't you run the rest of them through it."

I froze for a moment. Yes, I knew it. But I now had a dozen young women looking at me to take control of the situation. I wasn't ready. I was petrified. I realized this was the one time I would have to prove myself to them, and if I didn't get it right, I'd lose the girls for the entire season. All of a sudden, I realized I couldn't remember half of the girls' names. Who would I ask to call out the cheer? How would I correct the form if I couldn't remember names?

They say there is a first time for everything. And it's true! The first time always seems scary and intimidating. We feel as though we are not good enough and that we can't achieve the task at hand. But the fact of the matter is that once we get past the initial hiccups, everything works out just fine, and soon we are sailing our ship like we always knew how to. That is the beauty of life.

One of the girls I knew asked if she could lead it, so I gladly handed things off to her. I then went through the routine with them as they were doing it. They did it again, this time with me watching. I actually got to correct some form! I reminded some girls of timing and others on how to do the right K. We worked on the timing for our Ls. By the time the head coach came back, we looked a little better than we did when she left, and I didn't go running and screaming to the parking lot in shame! I had survived my first test as a "cheer coach."

After that first week, I made a couple of realizations. First, and no surprise, my daughter absolutely loved having me there. Some kids don't like having their parents so involved, but not my Anna. She seemed to enjoy us going to practice each night and then being able to talk to me about it all after it was over.

Second, it forced me to make some life choices. Up until cheer camp, my work schedule had been a bear. By August 1, I had flown more than 80 airline segments equaling nearly 90,000 miles traveled. I hadn't actually been home for an entire workweek at all during the calendar year. But with my commitment to the squad, I knew I needed to make some changes to my calendar. I would need to reduce the amount of travel I was doing and try to schedule around practices. I wouldn't be able to be at every practice, as work was obviously important, but I would do my best.

And third, I'd have to prioritize in other areas. My great stress reliever had been kickboxing. If not for work travel, I wanted to be on the mat five nights a week. But cheer training camp made that an impossibility. Monday through Wednesday, cheer directly conflicted with my training schedule. Thursdays would be tight, and even if I did make it, it would be an hour on the kickboxing mat after two hours of drills in the hot sun. But I made a commitment, and my commitment to the squad had to trump my personal preferences. So my own training took a backseat to cheer training.

Chapter 3

Facing my Fears

"Venture outside of your comfort zone. The rewards are worth it."

— Rapunzel, 'Tangled'

"Mandatory Coaches Clinic." When I saw these words for the first time, my whole body cringed. I hate the word mandatory; the more somebody told me to do something, the less I always wanted to do it. When I was younger and in school, I was one of the kids who always resisted anything that was required. For all four years in college, I skipped class as much as I could get away with, figuring I could learn all the material on my own. I am the sort of person who will take the online test before even reviewing the material, thinking that I will probably know enough to get by.

Being told that I had to spend an entire Sunday in August, starting at 7:30 am, in a community center gym to learn the finer points of coaching did not excite me.

It did not help that it was the same day my family was planning to go off to the beach, a fun trip that I would miss out on for this "mandatory" clinic. However, I did not want to be one of those coaches that blew it off, particularly as I was new to all of this and more so because I was the only guy coach in all of this. So I needed this clinic because I needed to learn about coaching, and if they were asking all coaches to go, I would be there. I would not be entirely happy about being there, but I would be there nonetheless.

I got to the clinic 15 minutes early for the 7:30 start time given to us, and in typical fashion, I was the first one there. I then learned my first valuable lesson of the day; the announced 7:30 am start time was not an actual time. It seems as if the community center itself did not even open until 8:30 am. As coaches from across the region started arriving at the community center at around 8:15, somebody explained to me that they always say 7:30, but that means nothing, and it always starts at 9. The experienced vets knew this. This newbie did not.

No surprise to me, but still nerve-wracking, I seemed to be the only male in a gym of more than 100 coaches. The one saving grace and upside to all this would be that I would not have to wait in line to use the restroom during breaks. There would be no insane rush for the urinals with this group of people. So maybe this could keep me going for now.

As people got ready and things were about to start happening, I went and sat with the other coaches, assistant coaches, and junior coaches from my community. These individuals would be coaching from Mighty Mite on up. I did not know where I belonged, so this seemed like the best fit for me at the moment, and they seemed to appreciate I was there. As I was new, I again went into listening mode, and I tried to learn as much as I could by taking in what they had to say and what they had experienced.

Being new, I was still trying to understand the coaching vocabulary, and I thought it was best not to open my mouth, not wanting to confirm my utter lack of understanding about what

I had gotten myself into.

After the first opening session, the clinic organizers broke the participants into smaller, more intimate groups. One room had been set aside to help everyone better understand the competitive scoring process and understand what judges would be looking for during the competition.

I had hoped I would have nothing to do with creating or scoring routines. Knowing that our experienced veteran coaches had that part down, I figured that was a session I could skip. Another room was set up to show tumbling, which was something I intended to watch later. In the third room, people were going through stretches and conditioning. This was where our head coach decided to stay for the time being, so I decided to stick around as well, and it also meant not having to leave my seat, which was a bonus.

The session in this room started quickly as the whole clinic's organizers had brought in a competitive squad of high school cheerleaders who were incredible at what they did. I could surprisingly follow many of the stretches and see both the value of them and how to demonstrate them to those I would be coaching.

I was starting to see the impact of the many different stretches and strength training depending on the girl's role, such as flyer, base, and back spot, and what use these could be to us. It was all starting to click into place for me, and I understood the purpose of all this. I could do this if I wanted to, and I did.

And then, just as I was starting to feel engaged and connected, something happened to abruptly remind me that I was still a fish out of water in this setting. We had a line of four or so teenage girls in front of us on the mat, demonstrating a flexibility stretch, lying flat on their backs with their legs spread eagle. Their coaches were urging them to continue to spread their legs as wide as they possibly could.

I was not sure how to handle myself. Not because I was not capable of being a professional, but because I was very aware that I was the only man in a room full of women and girls. I felt like a lecherous old man at that point, having to look at these girls doing these stretches with their legs wide open. I felt uncomfortable and did not know if I should be looking at this. I knew I had to be a coach, but I was nervous. The dad in me thought I needed to look away and instead just concentrate on the instructor talking to us.

At the same time, I thought about how disrespectful that would be to the athletes in front of us because they had trained hard and were only here to help us. How could I waste this opportunity and not learn from them? Fortunately for me, soon enough, the work on opening up their hips came to an end, and we moved onto something else far less nerve-wracking for me.

As I moved into watching the tumbling demonstrations, I found that my mind was wandering somewhere else. Before starting as a coach, I was advised by a lawyer friend that as a man working with and around young girls, likely having physical contact, even appropriately and with supervision, it would be in my best interest to get special insurance. After all, I did not want to lose my house and all of my family's life savings because of a cheerleader falsely accused me of doing something inappropriate. As a man working with young women, this was something I could not get out of my mind.

When first given the advice, I thought it was ridiculous and unnecessary. It was just another example of what was wrong with lawyers and with the legal profession. But I was now starting to see there may be some truth to it. Sure, I knew many of the cheerleaders and their moms, and they even liked me when I was a cheer dad in the stands.

What I did not know, though, was if the same sentiments carried over to me being on the sidelines and being a coach. Would they wonder why I wanted to be a coach? Would they think I had ulterior motives? It was one thing to be the cute team mascot in a tutu, making the moms laugh, but what would they, and their husbands, think about me working so closely with their daughters? Would they be watching me closely and keeping an eye on me? As the tumbling exhibition came to a close, I decided that I would make sure not to have physical contact with the girls during practice. I would not ever be alone with a girl either. Better safe than sorry, I thought.

The clinic was breaking for lunch when I was given a reprieve from my thoughts. My head coach was leaving, hoping to return to the beach to see her family. Unless I wanted to stick around, she told me, I should feel free to go as well. I jumped at the opportunity to leave.

I had a lot rattling around in my head due to the morning lessons, and I did not need more in there. I would instead take the afternoon to consider it all and figure out how I would move forward. I soon learned I was a complete idiot.

Weeks two and three of cheer camp meant one crucial thing to the girls – stunting and tumbling. The first week we mostly went through motions and cheer routines. Now we would be able to start doing cartwheels, round-offs, and walkovers. First, as stand-alone skills, and then as part of complete routines.

Before we could start, though, we had to test every girl to see what they could do. As some girls worked through their motions or particular cheers, we had one station to test tumbling. I was assigned to help the lead junior coach. We started with somersaults and slowly moved into more and more complex moves. We soon knew what each girl could do, what they could also not do, and where they needed the most help.

It was there that my very well-thought-out plan started to fall apart. One of the girls was insistent that she would do a back walkover but could not get it. She tried and tried and just could not kick over. So I was asked to spot her. With one hand on the small of her back and another guiding her feet over her head, we finally got her to do the move, but assisted by me. The cheerleader was thrilled. I was, however, starting to get worried. I was already breaking the rule I had set for myself.

And then all of the best-laid plans completely went out the window. After knowing where each girl was gymnastics-wise, we were now ready to begin actual stunting. Breaking the girls up in teams of four—a flyer, two bases, and a back spot—we could run them through lifts, catches, and the like to see where we were as a team. We could test the experienced girls to see if they could still do extensions and twists and other more complicated things.

So that's what we started to do, but of course, it didn't go smoothly. As the bases were lifting a flyer, they were not doing it in unison, so the flyer started to fall. And then I found myself catching girls before they fell to the ground. There was no amount of legal advice that would have led me to let girls just fall to the ground from three to five feet in the air when I could catch them. And so I caught them again. And again. And again. Different girls. Different falls. I was going around catching them one after another.

At the same time, to try and keep from falling, we were asking flyers to squeeze their cores and tighten their butts. And asking back spots to get the flyers up by grabbing their behinds. And I realized that I needed to get over myself and my politically correct hang-ups and just help these girls as any other coach would. But I did not know how to do that. I kept feeling like I was being inappropriate, even as I knew I wasn't.

Following the third week of practice, we had a cheer team pool party, and I found myself hanging out with the moms as usual, not a dad in sight. And I explained to one of the moms about the legal advice and then needing to catch her daughter repeatedly that week. She looked at me like I was a little crazy. Of course, she wanted me to catch her daughter; why would I even worry about that? At the same time, that mom then joked with another mom and me about "not telling the dads."

I then realized while I still needed to be aware of the potential issues, most of my troubles were unfounded. The other moms made me feel comfortable and helped me prioritize the needs of the girls and the team.

The second and third weeks of practice also helped me see my role a whole lot more clearly. I was never going to be an expert, one who could help the girls perfect their technique, but that was why we had junior coaches and why those junior coaches were so amazing. We also had a head coach who would motivate and push the girls, reminding them they could do better and they would do better.

What I could do was offer encouragement and help to boost the girls' self-esteem. I could tell each girl what a great job they were doing. When they had just learned something new, they would call over "Coach Pat" so they could show it to me and get their "atta girl." It was a new role for someone who is both an introvert and relatively pessimistic in life, but it was one I took on with gusto.

That also carried over into strength training. At the end of week three, we took the girls on a mile run to loosen up, and the head coach seemed a little surprised but grateful when I joined them on the run. Anna and I set off at a steady pace, but about halfway through the run, I noticed there was a cluster of girls far behind me. And since I run about as fast as a turtle in peanut butter, I started to slow down. Then I had Anna drop back to inform the laggards that none of them could "lose" to me.

The girls started to pick up their pace as I slowed mine down. As we approached the end of the run, I made sure each of those cheerleaders passed me. Each got the satisfaction of beating Coach Pat in a race. No matter how tired they were, they all won. And I was able to consider it a job well done for the evening. Whatever I lacked in skills and knowledge, I could make up for in encouragement.

With the entire squad – and an assortment of moms – sitting around a swimming pool on a lovely summer day in August, I finally started to feel like I was part of the team. For the first time, I was not feeling self-conscious about being the only man in the group. I was not feeling out of place or out of my element. No, I was not even close to being as knowledgeable as I would have hoped to be, but I was coming along. And I felt a sense of purpose with the squad.

In the passing weeks, I had gotten beyond the questions about "why" I was coaching. They knew I was doing it for Anna. I was realizing, though, that most of my attention during practice could not be on her. I was not only Anna's coach; I was there to help the entire squad. So I found myself focusing on other girls, often giving Anna less attention than I was giving others. But it seemed necessary because I didn't want to be accused of favoring my daughter.

Chatting with the moms, I followed my general approach to the first few weeks. I did a lot of smiling and a lot of nodding, and I listened. I offered a few contributions here and there. But it was not my place to dominate the conversation, particularly with women who knew each other well and may still not have known what to make of me.

Each day, we practiced on the football fields next to the football teams. I felt like I could feel the eyes of the football coaches on me with each practice, wondering what a guy who looks like me was doing with the cheerleaders. I should be coaching linemen, not flyers. Whether they were thinking it or not, I felt it each time the squads seemed to meet on the sidelines at practice.

It did not help to learn that for the first time, a woman was an assistant coach on one of our football teams. The early reports were that she seemed to be "fine" but was "awfully quiet," according to a conversation I listened in on. She was somewhat accepted into the "boy's club" because she was deeply passionate and knowledgeable about football. But what were they saying about me? What was the scuttle on the guy who was on the cheerleader sidelines? What was my scouting report? All I knew was that everyone, and I mean everyone, was aware there was a guy helping coach the cheerleading team this year.

Finally, we had a dad at one of the cheer practices, the father of one of our new girls. He watched the entire practice. As I glanced over, I wondered if he was here to check me out. Was he watching to see how I was interacting with his daughter? Was there something I needed to worry about?

For some, it may seem incredibly odd for an upper-middle-class white male to feel insecure and out of place. After all, we are the ones who are supposedly running the world. But as an introvert, I never feel entirely comfortable around people, especially when it comes to small talk. As someone who moved around the country quite a bit as a kid, I have never been incredibly close with people or trusting of new folks. As someone who once weighed more than 400 pounds, I am still enormously self-conscious of what people think when they see me and what they say about me. I am always going to assume the worst.

So when I looked at our squad, all those insecurities came through. I saw three junior coaches who were excellent cheerleaders in their own right. I saw three incredible women in our head and assistant coaches who could probably be cheerleaders even today. I saw amazing and determined young women throwing themselves into their sport. And then there was me—the weed in the middle of this beautiful garden.

Perhaps it is those insecurities that helped keep my focus on encouraging the team. In the first few weeks of practice, I kept explaining to Jen that I just did not get it. When I was in high school, the cheerleaders ruled the school. I looked at our squad, and I saw young women who are strong, smart, beautiful, and talented. They seemed to have the entire world in their hands. Yet, just about every one of them displayed major insecurities in one way or the other. I knew that if I could just put my issues aside, I could maybe help some of them with theirs.

Jen tried offering some psychological and sociological explanations, but it seemed too much for me. All I could see were 17 incredible girls who were putting themselves out there. Whether they won at the big competitions or not, each one was a rock star. And they needed to know that. If they could not believe it at age 10, there was no way they could hold onto it as adults with all they were doing. So I made up my mind that I was going to be a cheerleader for the cheerleaders.

It also meant that I would not give in to stereotypes, regardless of what I thought people might be thinking. Those who know me understand that I have walked around with painted toenails for years. When Anna was five years old, she asked me to go to the salon and get a pedicure with her. And we have done so each month since. Each month, she gets to pick my color. And no color is off-limits.

When I started kickboxing, which is done with bare feet, I got some strange looks at the gym. Some folks would ask what the orange, or pink, or blue toes were all about. Others likely had their less P.C. theories. But soon everyone realized that all that mattered was whether I could deliver an effective kick with my pretty, painted toes. And I could. In time, another guy or two would have painted toes on the mat, though they would tend to opt for chrome or black, not the reds and purples that Anna had chosen for me. I was used to doing things Anna chose for me, be it out of the ordinary or not.

So, as we were getting the girls ready with their uniforms, it also came time to order uniforms for the coaches. The first order was for regular coaching shirts, no problem. Then one of the assistants asked if we would get "blinged-out" shirts, coaching attire bedecked and bedazzled with all things sparkly. I quickly made clear that I was all in for the bedazzled coaching gear.

As the cheerleaders were discussing their uniforms for the coming season—new uniforms that had never previously been worn—one of the girls asked, "Coach Pat, are you going to be wearing a cheer uniform too?" I did not answer the question, but if the squad asked me to, and it meant supporting them, I knew that I would be there in a crop top and skirt too.

When training camp wrapped up, practice sessions were adapted to fit into a school year schedule. Yes, the summer training camp was tough. But the fall practice season was not going to be much easier. In addition to going to school, doing their homework, and engaging in any other sports and extracurricular activities, our girls were still expected to show up ready to work at cheer practice. The new schedule was two hours on Tuesday and Thursday evenings, two hours on

Saturday afternoons, and a one-hour optional tumbling clinic on Wednesday evenings. That was in addition to the Sunday afternoon football games where they were expected to be on the sidelines supporting the football teams.

I felt that I was getting to know the girls a little better with each practice, understanding them as people. And with each practice, I thought that they were coming to trust me just a little more. I could read the girls' faces to know who had a tough day at school or who was beginning to feel under the weather. I knew which girls would benefit the most from direct, concrete praise. I even knew which girls could be counted on, no matter how practice was going, who were the outspoken voices on the squad, and who would be the quiet leaders.

I had underestimated, though, how much Anna would need my help and support. Going into the season, I recognized I needed to be a coach for the entire team, not just for my daughter. That meant spending time with other girls, working with other stunt groups, and heaping praise on young women that were not in my family.

The previous season, Anna had been a flyer, and she relished the role. She enjoyed the spotlight, being the girl on top of the pyramid. It helped that she was flexible, with a strong core and natural gymnastics skills; she was built to be a flyer.

Her years of kickboxing training had also made her very strong, one of the strongest girls on the squad, both in her legs and in her upper body. So for Anna and her Junior Pee Wee squad, that meant one thing: we needed Anna as a base instead of a flyer.

The coaching staff tried to avoid making this decision for weeks, continuing to use her as a flyer at training camp. But in practices, we could see her stunt group struggling to hold her up for some formations. And we could see other groups having the same issue, with bases struggling to keep the stunts up. It wasn't that she was heavy, but more that the other girls just didn't have enough strength to effectively keep her in the air. We needed Anna to be strong, but at this point we needed her to be a strong base.

When we initially told Anna we needed to shift from a flyer to a base, she took it well. It meant a new level of learning for her and a new level of work. But it also meant a new level of frustration. She quickly got angry with a fellow base who she felt was not working as hard as she was. And she got mad with a flyer she felt was making her do all of the work.

Anna missed being in the spotlight, and I felt that I had not done a good enough job helping her see how vital the bases were and how valuable her contribution was. All she knew was that she was not one of the four flyers who were up in the air, where most people's eyes would gravitate to. She did not feel like she was contributing and began wondering why she even had to go to practice. "It's not like anyone would miss me," she would often say to me.

In all of the training I had to go through from the start of the season, there was almost nothing about coaching and motivating your own kids. I did not know how to explain to Anna that, while I may be spending all of my time in a given day with another stunt group, I was still paying attention to her out of the corner of my eye. I did not know how to deal with her meltdowns or overt frustrations. And I did not even know how to properly comfort her during practice without it looking like I was playing favorites.

Such perceptions did come into play, particularly with such young girls. After weeks of working through our routine, the coaching staff decided to make some changes to the dance part of the routine, including giving Anna a larger role in a tumbling sequence. Anna's larger role was a gut punch to another cheerleader whose role was being diminished. The change was made during one of the rare practices when the head coach was away and I was working with the girls.

The slighted girl immediately got angry with Anna, telling her that the only reason she was asked to tumble was because of me. While it was the furthest thing from the truth, there was nothing either Anna or I could do or say to dispel it. It was the perception she had, be it the truth or not.

Despite Anna's growing frustrations, she was a trooper, and she went to every practice, including the optional ones. She showed up at every game, and she settled into her new role as a base, a position she had not signed up for when she began the season. She took every curve ball we threw at her. And with each passing day, I was more and more proud of her.

Chapter 4

The Sleepover

"You're mad. Bonkers. Off your head ... But I'll tell you a secret ... some of the best people are."

— Alice in Wonderland

For most, when they think of cheerleaders, they think of them as young women yelling chants and shaking pompoms on the sidelines of football games. It is the image we have all come to associate with cheerleaders, whether it be rooted in our own high school experiences, what we saw at college, or what we see on the sidelines of NFL games today.

For our girls, Sunday football games were a loathed event. It was a bonding experience around how much everyone on our team hated these afternoons. We spent so much time during the season explaining to them that they were real athletes like these football players and as such, they needed to train, prepare, and focus as athletes would. Then Sundays would come around, and they could not do any of what they were training so hard for. They were severely limited in terms of stunting and tumbling because we were outside on the grass and not inside on mats. And so there they were, offering chants and shaking their pompoms on the sidelines. They hated Sundays.

Some weeks our Sunday games were at home and would be hosted at the local park. But many weeks, we needed to travel for the games, and sometimes that meant driving upwards of an hour each way. The season started with the weather being scorching hot, with our girls exhausted and dripping with sweat by the end of the game. But toward the end of the season, we were cheering at the games with the girls in their winter parkas, trying to stay warm as we attempted to motivate them with hot chocolate.

If anything, the Sunday games served as a bonding experience for the squad. It gave the girls time to hang out with and enjoy each others' company, dancing to the music that was played over the sound system, running to the snack bar at halftime for chicken fingers and cheese fries, and choosing cheers that would not disappoint their fellow squad members. I quickly realized there were some cheers the girls hated, particularly a few they had been doing since their starting days in cheer years before.

At the start of each game, if the opposing football team brought a cheer squad, it was customary that we would march over to the other side of the field to do our "hello cheer" for the visiting squad. Seventeen girls, three women, three teenagers, and me made the walk over to the other side each game.

Sure, we got some strange looks from people and the visiting teams, but I was growing more comfortable with each passing day and was starting to own my role as a cheer coach.

I even started to feel comfortable in our "cheer pen" on the sidelines. There, we would be doing our cheers, trying to rally the home crowd. And every week, I would be there, standing off to the side or sitting on a cheer bucket, watching over the girls and occasionally asking one of them to call a cheer.

When they called the cheer that required coach participation, I would be right there and was always ready to "get down" with the routine. And when they would go out to midfield at halftime to do their routine, I would be there on the grass, kneeling down and doing the eight counts to keep the girls together.

Because some of our girls were multi-sport athletes, they sometimes had to go to other practices on Sunday as well. A few played softball, and Sundays in the fall meant they could be playing two or three softball games that day, while trying to squeeze the football game in as well. With each passing week, I became amazed at the resilience of some of these girls. They would play two softball games and then rush over to cheer with their squad. These girls would be absolutely exhausted, but they were still going to be there for their fellow cheerleaders.

Most of the cheerleaders were participating in other activities, but they never let any of it affect their cheer practices.

At this point, I felt as if I had become a primary part of the group and helped the girls with their formations. I was getting more comfortable around them, and even though I was not the best at all the formations and I was nowhere nearly as good as the girls or the assistant coaches, I still could support them, and they started to rely on that support.

If they needed me for anything, I was always going to be there. I was glad that I had slowly become such an essential part of the team. I never thought I was capable enough, but they seemed to trust me.

The end of September meant that it was Anna's birthday. The year before, for her ninth birthday, she had decided to have her birthday party at our kickboxing gym, both because it was a place she loved to be at and because she wanted the chance to show off her skills to a bunch of her friends who had never seen her punch or do a round kick before.

Once the school year started, Jen and I asked Anna what she wanted to do for her birthday this year. We made a few suggestions, like going to the movies or taking a few of her close friends to the local amusement park. But none of our suggestions was good enough for her. As we got closer to her big day, she only had one thing on her mind, and she knew exactly what she wanted to do. A girl only turns ten once. She wanted to have a sleepover.

When I was a kid, my mother always insisted that my entire class needed to be invited to my birthday party, that it was not right to exclude a handful of kids. Whether I liked everyone or not, they were all invited to my birthday parties. And because of this, my parties were usually at our house or at a birthday joint like Chuck E. Cheese. It was always a little crazy with so many kids at one party, but it was still manageable. But a sleepover party was just a completely different beast.

Since a lot of Anna's friends were either on the cheerleading team or into a lot of other sports, it was tough to find a weekend that suited everyone. Just looking at the cheer schedule, my mind went a little dizzy because of how busy it was, but we managed to find a weekend that looked right, with just a home football game that Sunday and nothing else on the calendar. The next big issue was how many girls we should invite. It would be quite challenging to manage more than a couple ten-year-olds in one night.

Always the wise parent, Jennifer suggested that Anna should invite no more than three girls to the sleepover. But being the parent who had a difficult time saying no to people, and particularly to my daughter, I allowed Anna to double that, much to my wife's dismay.

So Anna and six of her friends came back to our house at 2 pm on a Saturday, immediately after cheer practice. The plan was they would stay over with us until we needed to head over to the local park for a 2 p.m. football game the next day. Which essentially meant 24 hours with seven ten-year-olds ruling our house. A genuinely terrifying concept for me (and our 12-year-old son, who escaped to his grandparents for the night), but having spent so much time coaching them, I thought I would be able to handle them for one night.

As Jen reached out to the moms to invite their daughters over, one actually asked, "Are you sure?" It was what we were all thinking, and she just said it out loud. Another told us that we were certifiably brave – and insane – for taking on such a task. A few other mothers offered to come over early Sunday morning to get their daughters if we needed the reprieve. Thankful for their concerns, we assured them that we would be okay.

The gaggle of girls proceeded to absolutely destroy our kitchen as they made slime (glitter slime!) and tore apart our bathroom while they did makeovers. They did stunts in the living room, doing their cheer routines for each other, and then together for (and with!) our family dog. They spent the night watching movies and ate a lot of pizza and candy. From what I could tell, they generally had a fantastic time as they took over the entire first floor of our home.

It was that weekend where I finally and truly started feeling comfortable in my role as a coach. Each one of those girls would regularly chat with me, to the point where I sometimes learned far more about their lives than I needed to. None of them were nervous or suspicious around the fat guy with the shaved head and the goatee. If they were comfortable around me, there was no reason for me to still be so afraid and uncomfortable around them.

And the same was true of the mothers, which made me feel better about it all. They all seemed completely fine with sending their daughters over to our house for the night. They said yes without any hesitation, and the fact that I was there was even a plus for them. (Jen was of course there the entire time as well, that was a given.)

One mother warned me that her daughter usually does not go to sleepovers, so I suggested that she could come over just for the afternoon and evening and that her mom could come to pick her up later that night. But by the time the pizza arrived, that girl had her mom running over her pajamas and a pillow so that she could spend the night with everyone else.

Sure, we might have been crazy for hosting seven ten-year-old girls in our house for an all-day sleepover, but seeing the girls enjoy themselves that evening and the next morning made it all worth it. I was not used to seeing any of them except Anna outside of practice, and we always pushed them hard at practice, and all of the girls took their roles very seriously. It was refreshing to see them in a completely different environment. To see them enjoying one another as friends and not just teammates was terrific. They were just having fun and being themselves.

After that weekend, Anna would regularly have some of her cheer friends over for sleepovers, though usually no more than one or two at a time. We had our limits with how many children we could handle at once on such a regular basis, but we loved that they loved our house. It became so normal that the girls would often just get dropped off without their moms even coming into the house to check on things before they left.

Both the cheerleaders and the cheer moms just trusted "Coach Pat," and this was something I was very proud of. Since I first started being Anna's coach, all I had ever wanted was for everyone to like me and not think of me differently because I was always the only man present. And this was the weekend when I knew I was a part of the team and felt good about it.

Chapter 5

Setting up the Base

"How do you spell love? You don't spell love. You feel it."

— Winnie the Pooh

    Our first competition for this season was nearing, and nerves were at an all-time high. There was a lot of pressure on us all, especially on the girls. By my count, the squad had been putting in about sixty hours of practice each month, and for girls that young, it was a lot of time. It was a lot of physical activity and a lot of direction and instruction. It was a lot of practice and a lot of repetition. It felt like too much for me; I can only imagine how our cheerleaders were feeling.

    The squad was less than a week from the first competition, and we still hadn't been able to hit our routine without mistakes. I could sense everyone's frustration because, as a whole, it just had not come together. Everyone knew their parts well, and each of them was excellent at what they did, but when performed together, we could not nail the routine. I could feel the tension in the atmosphere, and I just did not want them to give up.

    We were out of step, and we were making mistakes. Many times someone would get dropped. I had to remind everyone that the previous year it did not come together until the week before the competition, but I started to doubt my own wisdom. Our routine was far more complicated than the previous year's. I wondered if the girls would even be able to get it done. I knew they were great, and of course, I believed in them, but with how little time we had and how complicated the routine was, I had some doubts.

At the same time, my mind was somewhere else entirely. Before I had decided to be a coach, and before the intense cheer season had started, I had been a road warrior for work. I usually put in about 100,000 miles on airplanes in the first few months of the calendar year, but was behind my typical pace this year. Cheer practices were more hectic than I had ever anticipated, and they took up a lot of my time.

With cheer, I tried to minimize my work travel to be at as many practices as I possibly could attend, but I still had some travel to do.

The stress of all this was starting to get to me, though, and I was getting distracted by my work issues. I had hoped that my work pressures would not affect my coaching abilities, but I also needed to keep my job. A lot was bouncing around in my head. I had to figure out a way to balance both, but I wasn't sure how to.

Five days before the competition, I was at practice in a suit and tie, vastly different from my typical coach attire of shorts and a t-shirt. In all honesty and reality, I should have been in New York that day for work. Instead, I had arranged my calendar to be at practice that evening and then take a late evening train into the city for a bunch of upcoming meetings later that week. Most people at work thought I was insane to ditch work to coach a girl's cheerleading team practice, but they meant a lot to me. As their coach, I felt an obligation to be there for the squad; I wanted to be there to see them at the moment they finally nailed the entire routine.

This was not the night for that to happen. We had a rough start to practice as the girls did the routine in their full uniforms for the first time. There were numerous complaints about the uniforms, the crop tops were too tight, and the competition shoes did not have the right type of edges. Little things started to add up. Nothing seemed to be going right. We had more drops and mistakes than we had ever had. So the coaches decided to let the girls change out of their uniforms, and we would just work through it as we usually do. This routine was taking much longer than usual to learn, and I was getting antsy, both about missing work and the girls not getting the performance.

Anna, too, was not excited about being at practice that evening, and I knew this. It was evident that she had grown frustrated with some of her teammates not working as hard as possible because they were not getting simple steps she already knew how to do. As we tried to go through the routine again, I saw Anna do something she typically did not do. She usually was serious and focused on practice and executed every move perfectly, even if she hated her position. But today, she was moving and dancing all over the mat while she was holding her flyer up in the air. This was dangerous, and I was scared for the girl Anna was holding. The others in her stunt group were moving around as well, and as a result, they dropped their flyer. This was a clear signal that everyone needed a break.

We had the full squad stop for a water break and gave the fallen flyer a moment's rest before practicing again. I decided now was the perfect time to talk to Anna and went over and spoke to her about how she needed to stay steady and be more careful. We decided to bring her stunt group together to talk about and work on what went wrong. And that is when it happened, that was when I did the most horrendous thing I could ever imagine.

That was the moment I made my daughter cry.

After the break, I continued my conversation, but without really realizing I had started to raise my voice. And I chastised Anna for "dancing" and for forcing the other girls to move with her. I was purposely calling out Anna rather than anyone else because then maybe everyone would learn by example. I told her that she knew better and had to be more responsible, and that was when the tears came. I immediately regretted everything I had said, but it was too late.

Anna had started sobbing, and I stood there clueless as to what I should do now. I felt terrible. The head coach stepped in and offered her some encouraging words, and tried to console Anna. She also pulled me aside later and told me that it was not all Anna's fault. She was only moving because some of the other girls were too. While I knew that, I was trying to have Anna take charge of the group. I was also trying to model a tactic they had taught in one of my online coaching training sessions, where they suggested that coaches call out their children to correct everyone else's behaviors. Since it was introduced to us as part of the certification process, I thought it was a brilliant idea to try this with Anna. Was I ever wrong.

I had even previously talked about this exact thing with Anna, explaining that sometimes I may need to criticize her when I wanted to teach others a lesson. The logic behind this was that the other athletes would take it seriously if they see a coach call out her own child.

The thinking is wrong, and this technique did not work at all. I had been a nurturing coach who had just made his daughter cry. And I did not even know if the message got through to the few girls who needed it the most. I tried to talk to Anna, but she completely shut down and shut me out. I wanted to remind her about the coaching "tactic" we had discussed, but she had no interest in anything I said anymore. All she was trying to do was to not cry again.

I did not even know if she would want me to be her coach anymore after this incident. I would do whatever she wanted. I had yelled at her and embarrassed her in front of the entire team when she was one of the best out of all of them. I would understand if she no longer wanted me to be her coach.

I felt like the worst parent in the world. How could I possibly have done that to my daughter, who had been working so hard and was one of our best cheerleaders? How could I do that after asking her to change positions and learn a completely different side of cheer? How could I have done that? How could I be so nice to all the other girls but so cruel to my own daughter? Was she not the reason I started coaching in the first place? This was all I could think about anymore, and I no longer could maintain interest in the practice. I was stressed, I was distracted, and I felt horrible.

The minutes seemed to go by slowly. It was excruciating, and practice could not end soon enough. As we were finally wrapping up, I needed to leave the gym early to catch my train. And I had to leave knowing that, at that moment, my daughter hated me. I slinked away, wondering if I should ever come back, not wanting to ruin anything else for Anna. I did not want to leave while I was on bad terms with Anna, but I also had to go if I wanted to keep my job. I was miserable.

On my entire train ride to the city I thought about what I had done, and I thought about it for hours that evening. I had called her out in front of the whole team; of course, she hated me. I was unable to sleep, completely consumed with what a horrible thing I had done. The work issues that had preoccupied me earlier in the day were now the furthest thing from my mind. And I realized that work was not a priority; only Anna was. I felt terrible, and I would give anything to make amends.

That morning, I woke up and was still obsessed by thoughts of having made Anna cry. I did the only thing I could think of. I texted my daughter, not knowing if it had occupied her mind as much as it did mine.

"Can I tell you I'm sorry? I felt so bad about yelling last night. I was up all night. I love you and am so proud of you."

"It's okay, and thanks."

"I love you so so much."

"Love you too."

And with that, it was over. In the next few days, Anna and I would joke about what had happened. But I still remembered it because it was not a mistake I wanted to ever make again. I had been so good about encouraging all of the other girls on the team; how could I be so terrible about tending to my own child? Did I agree to coach for my daughter, or was I going to be consumed with winning? I never thought I would be the sort of parent who only cared about success, but now I was starting to worry. And I did not like it one bit.

Once all this drama was over, we still had two more practices left before the competition. On Thursday evening, we were using a high school gym that we had not previously used that summer, and the squad seemed to enjoy the change. It was new, and it was a better facility. And more than that, everyone seemed less stressed than they were at the last practice.

We rolled out all the mats and did some stretches, after which the girls went through the entire routine, AND THEY GOT IT! For the first time, they nailed it. We had them do it a second time, and they got it again. It was an incredible feeling.

Somehow, a switch had been flipped, and it all came together. It finally felt like our team was ready for the competition, and they could even win. But that was not even as important as the fact that they felt confident in the routine.

We did some tumbling drills and worked on just doing the actual cheer as loudly as possible, and we wrapped up the practice by doing the routine on our knees, for fun. The girls were in good spirits, and it seemed like they were ready for this.

Our final practice was on Saturday afternoon, and as expected once again, they nailed it. They chanted loudly and energetically. A few girls still needed help on some particular parts, but we felt confident competing as a squad. After all of the hard work, all of the mistakes, tears, and complaining, the girls were finally all smiling. They knew how strong they were, and they finally saw what they were capable of. And they felt great because of it, and so did I. I was proud of them.

The evening before the competition on Saturday evening, there was the ritual "curling party," where all of the cheerleaders came together to make sure each had the same curled hair for the competition the next morning. It was a ritual that allowed the girls to relax and enjoy each other's company and be friends outside of the gym while trying to offer a little routine for the night before when so many of them were getting nervous. It helped them bond and calm each other down, and in all honesty, it helped calm me as well; after all, it was going to be my first competition as a coach and not just a parent.

I was in charge of curling Anna's hair, which was an awful responsibility considering I still had no idea how. Like the previous year, one of the junior coaches took pity on me and offered to curl Anna's hair. I was grateful because I wanted Anna's hair to look perfect, and that was something I could not do. I would have just messed her hair up. Anna appreciated that it would be done right and that she had a high school junior helping her. Overall it was a good evening.

The year before, I had felt like the new guy just intruding at the curling party and had done my best to just blend into the furniture. This year was much different, since all of the moms knew me, and I knew all of their daughters very well. I was a part of the conversation, although I still did more listening than talking because that was what I enjoyed. But I felt like I belonged.

As many moms moved over to focus on the hair curling, I found myself talking to our head coach and a lovely woman who used to coach cheer. During our chat, I made a confession. While I had always realized that coaching girls cheer was difficult and challenging, I had no idea just how difficult and challenging it truly was. I thought coaches like them were amazing for what they did. The two just looked at me for a second and then smiled. I could tell that they realized I finally understood.

Before Anna and I left for the evening, the other coaches gave me a small gift – a black and orange feather boa for the competition the next day. Some may think it was silly, but I accepted it with pride because this coach would be honored to wear it.

Anna and I got home a little before 9 p.m., knowing we both probably needed to get some rest, but both of us had the sort of nervous energy that would prevent sleep. I got my backpack ready for the big competition the next day, making sure I had all the essentials: candy, hair ties, nail clippers, and basically anything I could think of to help the squad get through the day.

Anna was complaining about the coaching staff's decision not to let the girls bring their electronics to the arena the next day. We had everything laid out and ready to go and then finally decided that it was time to get some sleep. Tomorrow was a big day for both of us, and we needed all the rest we could get.

Anna was fast asleep within five minutes of her head hitting the pillow. With a handkerchief wrapped around her curled head, she had a great night of sleep. I wish I could say the same for myself. I had two alarms set so that we would not miss our 6:30 am wake-up call, but I didn't need an alarm. My nerves were all over the place, and it was an incredibly restless evening for me.

Chapter 6

The First Competition

"No matter how your heart is grieving, if you keep on believing, the dream that you wish will come true."

— Cinderella

After hours of tossing and turning in bed, I jolted myself fully awake at 4 am after a bad dream. I note that I never remember any of the dreams I have; I know that I have had a dream and that I must have dreamt, but I rarely wake up remembering anything, good or bad.

Surprisingly, this morning I did remember my dream. I dreamt about the competition and that our cheer squad was there but could not remember their routine. And so, with all the girls standing on the mat, not knowing what to do, we all just began doing the "Superman" cheer – the one cheer that almost every girl on the team absolutely detested. Waking from this nightmare was not the start to the day that I was hoping for.

This unusual morning continued when it was easier to wake Anna up that morning than ever. It usually would take me at least half an hour just to convince her to get out of bed, but today she got up quickly and immediately began to get ready. She even seemed to be in a good mood, until we were unable to find one of her cheer socks. She then struggled with deciding between her blanket or her panda onesie, and she did not know which one she wanted to bring with her to keep warm in the arena. To make our morning smoother, I just decided that it was easier if we opted for both.

We were ready and in the car by 7:15 a.m., and we reached the arena by 7:35 a.m. Given my track record, it was no surprise that we were the first from our squad to get there. Soon enough, the other girls began to trickle in and by 8 a.m., we had all 17 girls present. As we waited for the officials to open the arena, all the moms started removing the hair curlers from each girl's head. Finally, by 8:30 a.m., we all made our way through security and to our assigned section.

The West Windsor-Plainsboro (NJ) Wildcats were lucky to secure a prime spot in the arena this year. Our section was right near the entrance, which meant we did not have to go through the hassle of going up and down the stairs. And right behind us was a women's bathroom for the girls to use, which was convenient for us and made it easy to shuttle cheerleaders in and out.

Actually, to be more precise, what we had was not a women's room; it was a men's room that had been converted to a women's room for the competition. Before even getting to our seats, the girls had to use the bathroom. Most of them questioned why they were using toilets with urinals in them when the (temporary) sign outside said women's room.

When I searched for a restroom for myself, I later learned that for the half of the arena that served as "backstage" for the cheer teams, all of the bathrooms had been converted for the girls. And it made sense because I guess there was no real point in having men's rooms, even if that meant I was out of luck. I could wait – and walk to the other side of the arena – to go to the bathroom.

We only had a chance to sit in the arena as a squad for about 10 minutes before it was time to get up and start moving again. It was a full day. In those 10 minutes, the coaches double-checked every sneaker and managed to retie, with double knots as tight as possible, every shoe worn by every cheerleader.

We would not let there be any untied laces, or heaven forbid a flying shoe, as we actually had during our last practice; we would not let small things like laces take down our girls.

We marched our way down to the floor of the arena. The performance prep was a tedious process, and it was something I had not previously appreciated. We first had to wait on the outskirts of the floor, where we could stretch and begin to give the girls pep talks and take some photos of them.

From there, we moved backstage. First, we made everyone go on the stretching mat, where we went through our strength training and stretches to make sure each girl was loose and warm before we got started.

After that, we moved onto the tumbling mat, and we had each girl work on the gymnastic components of the routine. After a series of cartwheels, back walkovers, and back handsprings, we were ready to move onto the practice mat.

This was the last step in our warm-up before the real competition began. Here, the girls would walk through the routine one final time before finally performing it in front of the competition crowd. If there were any mistakes or last minute fumbles, they needed to happen here and now. If there were any problems, we could work them out here before the performance.

The biggest issue with practicing on the practice mat was our girls could not say the cheer as loudly as they needed to or as loud as they would have to during the real performance because other squads were competing on the other side of the curtain. So we went through the entire routine at half the usual volume. But I was proud of them because they nailed it! The routine looked great; we had no mistakes. We were as ready as we could be.

After all of this, we had to bring the girls to the "tunnel." This was the long runway between the practice area and the performance floor. We stood here and gave some final words of encouragement to the girls, and we did our group chant. I wanted them to be as excited as possible, so I did my best to motivate them. Many hugs were exchanged. Some of the girls looked nervous and almost like they would be ill, but all but one coach had to leave them. Those were the rules.

I joined the head coach and two junior coaches in a different tunnel. At the same time, one of our assistant coaches positioned herself to bring the music over to the music station. After what seemed like an eternity of just waiting and being far away from the girls, we were given our instructions. There were to be no signals to the girls, no eight counts, no interaction, and no photos or videos. All of this was strictly prohibited.

Without thinking, I flippantly asked, "Can I at least sing along with the music?" By the look on their faces, the judges were not amused.

And so we took our seats, which were right at the front of the stage. Us coaches held hands and waited for our girls to come out. The announcer called for the "West Windsor Plainsboro Junior Pee Wee Wildcats!" The squad confidently ran to their positions. It was game time.

It was only two and a half minutes, but two minutes and 30 seconds feels like an incredibly long time under these circumstances. From our practices, we knew that if they did not hit the first stunts during the cheer part, the entire routine would be off. One of our team leaders called the cheer to kick things off. The squad started off loud. They hit their first stunt, then the second. The volume of their chants started to decline, but they hit every move we had practiced.

We then moved into the dance portion of the routine, which was far more complicated. All four stunt groups got their twist up, and then the entire squad hit the pyramid. We had a few wobbles, but overall there were no mistakes, drops, or problems. And then just like that, they were done.

Whenever the girls did a stunt correctly at practice, I would automatically raise both of my arms into a touchdown motion. But here with my left hand occupied holding the head coach's right hand, I could not do that. But instead, with each successful move, my right hand went up, like Judd Nelson at the end of 'The Breakfast Club.' And each time, I could hear the parents behind us cheering loudly. I knew that our girls were getting it done.

After they were done, the squad quickly walked off the mat, and in our hurry, we ended up walking the wrong way! Instead of immediately joining our girls, we had to walk back through the congested bowels of the arena. At that moment, all I wanted to do was congratulate Anna, and I could not get to her fast enough.

And then it hit me. At several points in the routine, Anna was doing solo gymnastics in front of much of the squad. I had been so focused on making sure the team hit the stunts that I did not actually see Anna do what she did so well. I did not even know if she correctly did what she needed to do! I was so lost in the moment and so happy for the squad that I forgot all about her. As great as I felt as a coach, I felt awful as a dad.

We soon found the girls. They all had smiles on their faces, but none seemed to want to talk about the performance. Instead, they wanted to change out of their uncomfortable uniforms. So we brought them all to the bathroom. I stood outside alone, helping to direct newly dressed girls to those parents who were waiting on the other side of the gates.

By now, it was 10:30 a.m., and all the girls were getting hungry, so it was time to walk around the arena and see all the food options available for the squad. The stadium was nice enough to have one concession stand open for just the cheerleaders. The five girls with me were dissatisfied with the available choices and wanted to see what else the arena had to offer, so we continued our walk.

We passed through the gates and the metal barriers erected to keep the parents away from the team areas. Only cheerleaders and coaches were allowed beyond those gates. But on the public side of those barriers, we found the food we needed; after getting the much-needed smoothies, crab fries, and such, we headed back to our section.

That was where I was stopped because I was one of the only men here. Even with the five girls accompanying me, security stopped me and informed me that the area was just for teams and coaches. I had to point to my "Cheer Coach" polo shirt, after which I was allowed to pass. I had to point to that patch on my chest at least a half dozen more times that afternoon as I shuttled the girls back and forth.

After all of this excitement, the boredom set in. The Wildcats had to wait more than four hours until it was time to announce awards, and so we all waited with nothing much to do. And with our ban on electronics, it felt more like four weeks. We took out some moments from our boredom to cheer on the other squads from our town. The only way to spend this time was by going on many bathroom visits, trash dumps, and food runs.

Some of the girls chatted, some slept, and some watched the competition. I was nervous and was fidgeting with my phone, but I just was not into it. I wanted the results. With so much time on our hands and a lack of outcome, the coaches did what coaches do. We started to review and overanalyze our performance video. What did we do wrong? Where might we get the point deductions? How did our competitors do? What could we add to the routine if we were fortunate enough to move on? We even had outside "experts" (high school cheer coaches!) reviewing our video and those of our opponents to see if they could provide any insights into what might happen with the scoring.

Our head coach, who was also the cheer commissioner for our community, was called to the back just a little before 2 p.m. Suddenly the tension intensified, and you could feel the restlessness in everyone, but to distract ourselves, the coaches tried to make small talk. Then the competition announcer came to the microphone. The results were not immediate, and the suspense was extended because first they announced commercials for upcoming cheer events. It was followed by the selection of winners of the 50/50 raffle and gift baskets. And finally, they introduced the representatives from each of the communities competing. It was time to get down to business.

Our performance was very early in the day, but we had to wait a while until they announced the results of our category. We were aware that we had competed against very tough competition in our division, including from the previous year's national champion team.

All the Wildcats needed was to place first or second in our division. Either place would move us on to regionals. Finally, our category was announced, and we held each other's hands. My hands were being squeezed so tightly that had I not been so lost in the results, it might have hurt. But the announcement came down; second place went to the West Windsor Junior Pee Wee Wildcats! We did it! We had advanced.

I cannot tell you the last time I have been so excited. I was elated. Entering the arena earlier in the day, I was more nervous than I had been in a long while. I looked around at our girls, and they were brimming with happiness, grinning from ear to ear, jumping up and down.

I rushed to hug one of my fellow coaches; it all felt so surreal. Then I saw one girl just completely break down into tears, and she was sobbing with joy and just could not contain herself. After working so hard and focusing herself so much on this, she had done it. We all had. Finally, one of the junior coaches went to the girl, picked her up, and cradled her until she stopped crying and composed herself. But she was expressing what we were all feeling.

Our head coach soon found us and was carrying our trophy. All the girls wanted to touch it. We got a group photo with the trophy. Parents started gathering around to congratulate us. It was a very happy afternoon, much better than I had remembered from the previous year.

While I do not believe I did a lot to help us achieve the win, I was just glad to have had the chance to be a part of this team and to be able to share it with Anna. It was a very special day.

After we said our goodbyes, Anna and I got ready to head over to my parents' house. My mother had been at the competition to watch Anna, and we had decided we would all get together for dinner that evening. Once in the car, Anna told me that she wanted to spend extra time working on her back handspring in the coming weeks. "I need to get it for [Head] Coach Chris."

This was the same girl who had been fighting against the back handspring for weeks and had tried to avoid it as much as possible. She had even asked to skip the extra tumbling practice out of fear that she would be expected to do it. Now she wanted to do it for her team. I was so proud of her, but I thought it was best to let her sleep on it before telling anyone else she was going to try.

Anna was so tired from the day that she fell asleep at dinner and once again in the car on our way back home. We reached home by 6 p.m., which by no means was late, but it had been a long day for both of us. I let her sleep for another few hours on the couch before finally heading to bed. Anna slept very well that evening, and so did I. The girls had worked so hard all those months, and I just wanted to see them succeed. And now they had. They won.

But our journey had just begun, and we had to work harder than ever before after this win. Regionals were in less than a month, and it was the only thing standing between us and a trip to Disney for Nationals.

Chapter 7

Showmanship

"A true hero isn't measured by the size of his strength, but by the strength of his heart."

— Hercules

One would think that the enthusiasm and excitement from the last win and the next competition would be enough motivation to carry the girls for the next month. They had already done a fantastic job competing against some of the best cheer teams in New Jersey. They had seen all that was possible and saw the strength and potential in their teammates. But when we all returned to practice the next week, we found our girls nothing but bored and frustrated.

In a sense, I understood where it came from. For two and a half months continuously, they worked and worked on the same routine and nothing else. And they had nailed that routine at the competition. But now it was time for the coaches to be nit-picky about what could have been better. To advance to the next level, we had to fix every little bobble and get every individual point possible.

While we had done amazingly at the competition and had no drops, no significant problems, and no penalties or deductions on our scorecard, there were still areas where we could clearly do better. While our dance routine was challenging and was executed well, it did not impress the judges enough. We were technically quite strong but lacked the showmanship that some of the top teams had.

We definitely knew we needed to add additional moves to the routine, and we had to do this by pushing our stunt groups harder and looking to pick up points wherever we could. But the biggest issue was that the girls were not as invested anymore, they were bored. After all the build up to the first competition, they were burnt out, and they were having trouble reengaging. We needed to have the full attention of our girls if we were to improve. We needed to bring in someone they would listen to and respect because of their knowledge of cheer.

Fortunately for us, one of our flyers' aunts was a former college cheerleader and a high school coach. The second practice after the competition, she came in to talk to the girls and try to motivate them with some tough love. She spoke to them about the importance of respect and how the girls needed to pay attention to what their head coach was telling them. She declared that if she was their coach and they disrespected her like they were currently disrespecting their coaches, she would have had them do laps until their legs fell off. She was making us look great in comparison.

Our "motivational speaker" preached the importance of sharp and clean motions, flyers holding a stronger core, stunt groups pushing harder, and generally taking practice more seriously than she was seeing. The response was excellent, as some girls wanted to demonstrate that they could do what this woman was asking for. A few of them struggled with this tough "drill sergeant" approach. For weeks, I was asked by some girls, "Will the mean lady be coming back?"

As a coaching staff, we needed to make some drastic changes and decided that somehow we had to make practices more fun than they had been. All season, we were having issues with getting all of the girls to attend each practice, and all these absences were having a severe impact on certain stunt groups.

So we instituted a reward system. For each practice or game where all 17 girls were present and prepared to practice, they would earn a letter. Once they spelled WILDCATS, they would earn a major team reward.

These incentives seemed to work. Slowly but surely, they were building up to "Wildcats." There was a setback where one of the girls came to practice in flip-flops, and there was no extra pair of sneakers to be found anywhere for her. We even tried to see if any of the coaches' shoes would fit her feet, but in the end, she finally had to sit the practice out and just watch for her safety. No letter could be earned that day, despite perfect attendance.

When we finally spelled the full word, the girls received a party on a Sunday afternoon, and it was just what everyone needed. It was the perfect time to bond with each other without any stress of practice and competition. The girls played carnival games and stuffed their faces with junk food.

They took tons of selfies with each other and what was even better was that they even went off into corners to stunt and do other cheer things on their own. They were 10-year-old girls again just for the afternoon, and they were better off for it.

This afternoon was useful not just for the girls but also for the coaches to see that we needed to shake things up in practice. Doing the same thing repeatedly and hoping for different reactions, results, and excitement from the girls was insane and unreasonable.

So it was decided we had to make practice more fun. Some of the basic warm-ups were replaced with dance parties. And we started a new system where we started awarding "tickets" to the girls when they achieved their goals, and those tickets could be used to bid on prizes right before the regional competition.

Soon after we changed things up, we saw an immediate response, and the girls were working harder and putting in more effort, all in the name of those little tickets. Each girl kept meticulous track of how many tickets they earned over the weeks. I could not say the same thing for the coaches, though; I know I lost track after the first day.

We even added an extra tumbling class for those girls who we thought could push through and execute back handsprings, and this was a move that could gain us additional points on the score sheet. Anna was one of the five girls who participated.

My daughter gave it her all, she really did, but in the end, lacked the confidence to do it during the competition. She knew she could hit the move on the mat during practice, but she was just afraid of failing during the competition. She just did not want to let her squad down.

Finally, the big weekend arrived – Eastern Regionals. The girls were as ready and prepared as they possibly could be. On the evening before, as was tradition, we had another curling party, complete with a raffle for an assortment of prizes. Each girl was given the tickets they had earned in practice over the last month to put into drawings for the prizes. Every girl left with at least one award, with some trading and bartering one prize for another.

Thankfully, our willing junior coach again curled Anna's hair (Erin, I will always be so thankful for your kindness at these parties and your commitment to the squad and the coaching staff over the years). We repeated the same process before the previous competition, with Anna's hair in curlers and a handkerchief and her in bed just minutes after we got home from the party. Even though this was no longer my first competition, I was still nervous.

On Saturday morning, we repeated the process from the previous month. Anna was in her uniform and a onesie before we left the house. We were off to the same arena and went through the same check-in process as a month earlier. Only this time, it was much colder outside (it was now mid-November) as we waited for all of our girls to arrive.

The one challenge that arose for me was that it was the same day as my grandmother's 100th birthday party. It was essential to my family that Anna and I be with them for the party. But I felt it was just as crucial for Anna to be with her team when the competition results were announced.

While Jen and our son, Michael, would be able to leave after Anna's performance and make the one-hour drive to my grandmother's party with plenty of time to spare, I really thought Anna should be there with her team, and I insisted she would need to wait until the scores were announced.

One of our coaches offered to take Anna home after the awards, but I really wanted Anna both up at the family party AND at the arena with her team; this was an experience they should share. So I made the executive decision that we would wait for awards, be with the team, and then make a hasty exit and go to the party and attend as much of it as possible.

We repeated our arena routine that morning, retying everyone's shoes, inspecting uniforms, and trimming fingernails. We went through the morning walkthroughs, stretching and tumbling and doing the routine one final time. We had definitely made the routine harder over the last few weeks, but the girls had this. They were talented and confident. They could do this; I believed in them.

As we said goodbye to the squad and waited for them to take the floor, my stomach was already in knots. We had come in second place at Central Jersey, and our girls were certain that they could never beat the team in the first place, no matter how hard they tried or how well they performed. Even before they hit the floor, in their heads, they were already competing for second place. And that is just no way to compete. I wanted them to believe in themselves just like I believed in them.

The Wildcats were introduced, and our girls came out onto the mat. They were full of energy and hit their stunts. They did their dance and were absolutely fantastic. I was so proud of them and all that they had achieved. As I raised my arms in celebration, I was almost sure we would be moving on to Disney and the Nationals.

But I knew enough about cheer at that point to know that what I thought and what I felt had little bearing on reality. It was all up to the judges. We had done the best job we could. All we could do now was wait for the results, which for me was always the worst part. And I had to keep an eye on the clock to make sure I would make it to my grandmother's party before it was too late.

The hours seemed to drag on, and there were only so many trips to the ladies' room, to the concession stands, and to the photo terminals I could make. I was so worn out by the season that I just was not up for any small talk. I was jittery and nervous, and I needed the results.

The AV system for Regionals seemed to be significantly worse than it was for Central Jersey. As they started making their way through the awards, it was hard to understand which category was being awarded. We heard the second place announcement for another squad, but no one was quite sure if it was for our grouping. They then announced the first place, and it went to the same team that topped us in Central Jersey. And that is when I realized that our season was over. We would not be advancing to Nationals.

Most of us had not even realized it was our category that was just announced. It was only when they saw the fan section of our rivals exploding that it all sunk in. The Wildcats had lost. Some of the girls started crying, and some of them started hugging each other. They all slowly began to pack up their things so that they could find their parents.

With our head coach on the floor for awards, I found myself trying to guide the majority of our squad through the arena to the parent area. I was sad that we had not won, and I was also worried about making it to my grandmother's party on time. But I realized this loss was severe, that we all needed a moment. So I pulled all of the girls off to the side so I could talk to them. I told them that they should be proud of their hard work and commitment because I was. I told them what an honor it was working with them, and I could not have imagined coaching a better team.

I kept it short, as I was already trying to fight back the tears. But I needed all of them to know that it was okay to be disappointed, but they should not be too sad. They needed to see all that they achieved because they had accomplished a lot.

After handing off cheerleaders to their moms, Anna and I quickly got into our car and traveled north to my grandmother's birthday party, making it just in time for the cake. There, I had to tell family member after family member that our season was over. I felt a bit numb about it all.

I felt bad for missing a lot of the party, even more so when my grandmother passed away five months later, and, despite my previous words, I felt terrible for the squad as well. After all of the hard work they had done, they deserved to move forward. We deserved to move forward. But I guess it just was not meant to be.

Chapter 8

Jersey Wild

"Love is putting someone else's needs before yours."

— Olaf, 'Frozen'

For months, I had known what my schedule looked like, and I had a routine that I loved. If we had won at Regionals, we would have less than a month to prepare for Nationals, and life would have been hectic with cheer practice. But if we lost, then our season was over. I knew this, I thought I was prepared for whatever the result would be, but when it actually happened, I realized I was not ready for such an abrupt end to our season.

For three and a half months, I had spent ten or so hours a week with these girls, and we were like a big family. I had spent at least the same amount of time and thousands of text messages strategizing with my fellow coaches. We had spent more than 100 hours practicing, and just like that, it was all over. No practices. No routines. No water breaks. No smiles. No exhaustion. There was nothing, and suddenly, my days felt empty.

I wanted to keep Anna motivated and involved, and not to let this defeat get her down, so I started taking Anna to open tumble at the local gym. We would run into some of my girls there, and each time I saw them, it would warm my heart and make me nostalgic for cheer season. Yet seeing them also made me sad, feeling that I had somehow let them down. Each girl would talk about getting ready for next season, showing a level of optimism that I wish I had.

I did not even know if Anna would want to return to the Wildcats the following season, and worse, I did not know if she would want me back as a coach. And I certainly did not know if the other coaches would want me back. But it was too soon to worry about all of that; there was a lot of time until next season, too much time.

Before Regionals, the cheer moms had given the coaches a gift certificate to a local restaurant as a thank you for all of our work. On the Saturday of Thanksgiving weekend, the four adult coaches met up for dinner. I had no idea what to expect from this dinner, I was nervous, and a part of me was trying to find an excuse for not showing up in the first place.

We welcomed each other with hugs and started talking about cheer and how much we missed it. We talked about the holidays, and our families, and everything else about our lives. Time flew by, and we ended up spending nearly five hours at dinner that evening. It was one of the most fun and relaxing evenings I had had in quite some time. Despite both Jen and Anna teasing me about my "girls' night," I realized I had missed being around these people who had accepted me as one of their own. I was glad that I had not skipped the dinner and comforted to realize that I got along with all the coaches even when we were not practicing for a competition.

That evening I realized just how big of an impact the season had had on me. I loved the girls on my squad like my own daughters, and I loved my fellow coaches like my family. With each passing week, no matter what happened, they were there for me, and I tried my best to be there for them as well. They took me on as a new and inexperienced coach when they did not need to and accepted me into the club. No matter what happened next, for them to even give me this opportunity in the first place, I would be eternally grateful.

As we hit December, Anna continued to do open tumbling at the local gym. I was aware of the fact that the gym was home to the Jersey Wild, an all-star cheer squad, but I had little to no knowledge about what that was or what all-star cheer meant. But I knew the gym had a lot of trophies and banners to show for its efforts.

Knowing how Anna could be completely fickle about her athletic pursuits, Jen and I were a little taken aback when Anna asked us if she could try out for Jersey Wild. We were both unsure about this because the Wildcats season had been an emotional one, and Jen and I both thought a break from cheer might actually be a good thing for Anna. A break from countless practices, anxious nerves and competitions, and, often, the emotions of defeat.

But I did not want to say no to her, as I never could, so I decided to humor Anna and at least explore the idea. We first learned that Jersey Wild was very expensive; it would cost us thousands of dollars for a "half-season," running from January to April. We also realized that Jersey Wild was strict, far more than the Wildcats ever were.

Anna would be attending more practices that winter than she had in the fall for the Wildcats. And if she missed three practices, she would be instantly kicked off the squad. It meant that we would not be able to go away for winter or spring break. For four months, her life would need to revolve around the Jersey Wild team, practices, and competitions.

This all sounded tough, but despite all of that, Anna insisted it was what she wanted to do. There was nothing we could do to stop her, so we let her try out. The Jersey Wild staff knew Anna from the Wildcat practices in the same gym. They saw in her all of the skill and determination that I knew she had. Without even taking a moment to consider, they offered her a spot on the squad. And they offered her a role that would allow her to return to being a flyer, a position where Anna shined brightest.

Over the course of those four months, Anna had four competitions. Before the first competition in Atlantic City, we received notice about the "look" she was expected to have for the team and the competition. Jersey Wild's look was much different from what we were used to or even comfortable with on Wildcats. We had already purchased the sparkly and revealing cheer uniform assigned by Jersey Wild. Now we were told our 10-year-old would need to wear her hair in a teased high pony and that she would be expected to have a "smoky purple eye" and bright red lips at every competition.

I did not know how to feel about this because we had preached to our Wildcats that they were athletes first and foremost. When our girls asked us about wearing makeup at the competition, as some of the other teams did, we would tell them that professional soccer players do not dress up in full glam for their games. It was not part of cheer for us, and it did nothing to enhance their skills. We did not do makeup. But now, I had to prep my daughter like she was a Miss America contestant.

Jersey Wild was not just a single team. They had many squads that participated in these competitions, including an elite year-long squad, Anna's squad, and several teams for older or younger girls or those with a lower level of difficulty. But all squads looked the same, and all of them competed in full makeup.

The area where the Wildcats always lost points was our showmanship. Technically, we were an excellent squad, but we lacked the sizzle or sass that some of our competitors had. This definitely was not an issue with Jersey Wild.

Parents were forbidden from attending any of the Jersey Wild's practices, which was new for me since I was so used to being her coach, and I missed it. So when Anna was at practice, I would often work out in the gym in hopes of catching a glimpse of her at practice. From time to time, I would try to peek through the covered windows to see what they were doing. Right before every competition, they would let parents see the routine once, as long as we did not take any pictures or videos of their routine.

They were strict about everything, and I did not understand the logic behind a lot of these rules, but it seemed like it worked for them, so maybe I shouldn't be one to question their methods.

I may not have enjoyed it as much, but clearly, Anna was having a great time, and that was all that mattered. She was tumbling, dancing, and stunting like she was born to do it. At three of the four competitions she participated in, her team walked away as grand champion. But I could not help but notice that they approached their routines very differently from how the Wildcats did. The Jersey Wild team was in constant motion, and things happened so fast that one would not know if a mistake was made or a bobble happened unless one was specifically looking for it. It was so fast that you could not really see any small mistakes.

It made for an entertaining routine, but it lacked the precision we had preached with our girls. But the Jersey Wild teams were champions, so maybe they knew better than I did.

Throughout her Jersey Wild season, Anna had quickly developed some close friendships with many of her new teammates. I was also friendly with their moms whenever we waited for practice to end, although I never quite developed the sort of friendships that I had with the Wildcat parents. It just did not feel the same, and maybe it was because I was less involved with the team than I was with the Wildcats.

At the end of each practice, Anna would bombard me with stories in the car about which girls had screwed up in practice, which girls got yelled at by the coaches, and which girls cried. It seemed the squad's head coach's approach to teaching was to scream, yell, and make the girls emotional wrecks; it was the exact opposite of how I had approached coaching, I hated raising my voice to them, and I never wanted to make them cry. At least not again.

None of the girls liked their head coach, in fact, they were all afraid of him, but they performed well out of this fear. All of this made me wonder if it was indeed better to be feared than loved. But I knew deep down that I could never be the type of coach who was okay with being disliked; I would rather not have any of the girls hate me, they were like my own daughters.

As Anna and Jersey Wild prepared for their final competition, for their version of Nationals, Anna began asking if she could join the full-year Jersey Wild squad instead of going back to the Wildcats. Anna liked winning, and Jersey Wild was good at winning. She liked working hard and having everyone around her work just as hard. She liked the makeup. And she liked flying.

But I explained to her that she had already committed to rejoining the Wildcats for the 2018 season and that she needed to fulfill that promise. If she really wanted to do Jersey Wild, she could do it after the next Wildcats season was over, in a half-year team again. Anna was visibly disappointed, but she understood and did not want to let anyone down either.

At the last Jersey Wild competition, Anna left as a champion. She was ecstatic and on top of the world. All she did was talk about the next season with the Jersey Wild squad and about all of the friends she had made in Hillsborough, a New Jersey community about a half-hour away from us. A number of Hillsborough girls had commuted down to be on the Jersey Wild team that winter. Anna even asked if we could move to Hillsborough or if she could at least join their Pop Warner cheer squad instead of Wildcats. She had made up her mind to continue cheerleading; for her, it now was just a matter of where and with what squad.

Anna mostly wanted to be a Jersey Wild, and if not, she wanted to become a Hillsborough Duke like so many of her Jersey Wild friends. And if neither of those two was possible, she would reluctantly return to being a Wildcat, but either way, she would continue cheerleading. I was happy that she had found a sport that she was so dedicated to, even if it meant her being on a more competitive squad with me not being her coach.

A week after her final Jersey Wild competition, I took Anna over to the gym for another open tumble session. We reached the gym only to find that the cheer room had been chained and padlocked. A sign on the door simply said that there would be no open tumble.

A few days later, we received an email from Jersey Wild, announcing that the gym had kicked them out, and as a result, the entire program, including Anna's squad, was being disbanded. A few days after the email, the gym posted an announcement on its Facebook page that they decided to break up with the Jersey Wild squad because it wanted to use the cheer space for something that could be used by a larger number of its gym members.

Anna was quite upset about all this because of how much she liked being on the team that was winning. For Anna's sake, I thought I should find out what really happened, but when pressed for additional details, neither the former staff of Jersey Wild nor the gym would provide any answers. The cheer space was still unused seven months later, with all of the Jersey Wild banners and trophies still in the room. But the program was nothing more than a memory.

The dissolution of the Jersey Wild program allowed me to see just how incredible a cheerleader Anna really was, and that she was meant to do this sport. Everyone else seemed to have realized this before me, and before that last competition, some of the Hillsborough moms had started talking to me about how lovely their community was and how good the schools in that area were. They even offered to share driving shortcuts that would allow me to get from Hillsborough to my work in Princeton in no time at all.

Friends shared Zillow listings with Anna of houses we could buy in Hillsborough and let Anna be on the team. They even talked to me about whether I wanted to negotiate an "out" with the WWP Wildcats so that Anna could become a Hillsborough Duke; I had folks willing to help with everything just so that Anna could be on their team.

This was all because Anna was an outstanding flyer.It was all a little overwhelming, to say the least. Even over the summer, Anna received a long impassioned text from a friend asking her to please move to Hillsborough because, in her view, without Anna, their cheer squad would be "screwed." How had I not realized earlier just how good Anna was? No wonder she liked the Jersey Wild, she was a winner, and she was one of the best cheerleaders there was.

But as Jersey Wild came to an end, Anna received more than just interest from the Dukes. Over a period of two months, Anna was "recruited" by at least half a dozen more all-star squads, all with flyer positions and all wanting to see if Anna wanted to join their squads. The amount of attention Anna was getting was surreal. Some of the teams interested had gyms an hour away from us, and some were charging more than $10,000 to join the team. (At this level, there were no skill-based scholarships; we would get to pay for the privilege of her joining their teams.) All this interest in my 10-year-old daughter because she was comfortable and confident at the top of the pyramid.

Anna was flattered by the attention, and she would ask us about each and every text or inquiry she received and whether she could join. But each time, I reminded her of one simple fact, that we are Wildcats. She had a promise to keep and a team to return to.

Section 2

Succeeding in Adversity

Chapter 9

Losing a Quarter of the Squad

"Change is good."

— Rafiki, 'The Lion King'

    I had thought that returning to the Wildcats in the fall would be exactly like it had been before, that everything would return back to normal, and we would get back to practice as usual. I had been itching to be a coach again to all the girls and to Anna, but I had not realized that nothing could be like it was. Little did I know this year was going to be very different and far more challenging than I had ever anticipated.

    Our team from my first coaching season, my original squad, had to be broken up and separated. It felt terrible because we were like a family; I had not realized that we would be on different teams this next year. Our younger girls had to stay behind on the Junior Pee Wee squad while Anna and the older girls moved up to become the Pee Wee team. To make up for this loss, we added four girls who had previously been on the JV squad, an older group ahead of us, who had not yet aged out of the program as their teammates had. We also added two new girls who had never cheered before but wanted to try. I embraced the idea of welcoming new girls to the squad and to the sport; after all, the coaches had given an inexperienced and new coach like me a chance, so I owed it to them to do the same for the team.

Training camp this season was much like the first season, four nights a week in the park. The girls were extremely anxious to get started on the work that they wanted to do. There was nervousness about what was to come.

But this was not all that was new and unexpected this year. What we did not expect was that several girls, almost a quarter of our squad, would actually quit during training camp, due to injuries, bat mitzvah prep, and various personal issues. All this forced us to rethink our plans earlier than we usually would in the season. Would we even be able to compete anymore? Should we still compete, considering we were so many members down? There was definitely a lot to think about.

These dropouts also sadly resulted in reductions to the coaching staff. As girls left the team, so of course did their mothers. We entered training camp as a coaching staff of five, but by the the end of August we were down to a coaching staff of merely three.

Despite all this change and loss, we persevered, and all in all, our fall practices went well, much better than I expected. The hardest part of all of this was keeping the girls off their phones. We got to the point where we actually needed to confiscate all cell phones at the start of practice just so we could hold their attention. When they were on their phones, their usually incredible performance suffered, with many stumbles and wobbles that were unnecessary and completely avoidable if the phones were not present.

This was a decision that was met with many unhappy faces on the squad because what teenagers like to be kept away from their phones? But this was for the best of the team.

This time the girls were all a little older and all a little stronger, so technically, we were a better squad. When we wanted to work, we could do a great job. But it was hard to get the girls to focus on working. Their attention was often elsewhere, particularly since most of the girls had just started middle school that fall, and there was a lot of newfound drama in their lives. The majority of the squad were now sixth graders, and the issues they had in school were carrying over to their practices.

The girls spent a lot of time at practice together like they did any such season; in August, it would be two hours a day, four days a week, and in September, it would be three days a week and a football game every Sunday. It was a lot of time together and a lot of time spent practicing, so if they did not pay attention, it all really turned out to be a disaster. It reflected poorly on us as coaches and on the girls; they were excellent cheerleaders, just ones that lacked focus.

On several occasions, we had to tell them if they did not want this, we could just quit now; we were getting ready for Central Jersey, and at this level, we had tough competition. It was going to be much harder than the previous year to advance in our division. There was no point if they did not even want this. They were great, and I knew they could be even better, but we had to make sure that they were at their best for the competition.

I feared that all this would mean Anna would get frustrated because of how happy she had been with Jersey Wild and the allure of the other teams; she had just spent months as part of a team that won competition after competition. Now here she was in a team where we had lost a quarter of our cheerleaders and coaching staff, and where our focus was at an all-time low.

This could be detrimental for the competition, which was looming. I knew the Wildcats could be just as good as any other team, and they had heart, but they needed to focus if we wanted to win. I wanted the best for the team and for Anna. Even though we had lost a considerable part of our old squad and were down many members, we kept on going, I knew we could do well if we all really tried.

Soon enough, it was the middle of October which meant it was time for the Central Jersey competition. The last time we had been in this arena was when we lost at Eastern Regionals the year prior. This time though, we came in absolutely sure about ourselves. We really thought we could win, but we also knew that anything could happen.

Cheer is an incredibly subjective sport, and you have a two and a half minute routine to make it all happen, or have it all fall apart. Then you have to leave it all up to the judges and hope that they saw all that you did and how well you performed, that they did not see your problems, and that they give you the score that you truly deserve.

The Thursday before the Central Jersey competition, we thankfully managed to hit our routine perfectly at our last practice. It was the first time we had been able to do that all season. We took that as a sign that we were ready for what was ahead.

And we really were. Our warm-up was just as strong as our last practice. I wanted to get them in a good frame of mind before it was time to perform, I wanted them to be at their best and not to be nervous, and all the girls seemed relaxed and ready. They were prepared. There was not much more I could do. After getting through the warmup exercises and routine, it was time for the girls to enter the tunnel. The head coach, me, and our junior coaches had to say our goodbyes.

We left the girls to prepare to make their way to the mat. We went to take our places, so we could cheer them on from the folding chairs right in front of the audience.

Just as I had hoped and expected, my Wildcats were absolutely fantastic. Everything they did seemed to go right that morning. The routine was absolutely flawless, and even I could not spot anything wrong with it. The crowd was into it, and the girls felt it. I jumped almost 10 feet into the air after it was over, celebrating how well we did.

After we left the mat, we brought the squad over to meet their parents and prepare for the awards. Hours of waiting later, it was finally time to hear the judges' decision; even though we had done great, it was still a nerve-wracking wait. It always was.

The announcement came down: WWP Pee Wee Wildcats took First Place at Central Jersey! For our girls, this was the first time that they had ever taken first place. They were on cloud nine because this was a significant achievement. And it was the first step down the path to Disney and Nationals.

Chapter 10

Disney Dream Crushed

"Oh yes, the past can hurt. But the way I see it, you can either run from it or learn from it."

— Rafiki, 'The Lion King'

The win was new to the girls and to me; they were ecstatic and already thinking about getting to Nationals and Disney. That had always been the dream, but now it did not seem so far out of our reach.

The first-place finish also meant that we had earned a spot to compete at Globals, a new competition launched just the year before by YCADA, the governing body for youth cheer.

YCADA had timed it so that it would happen about six weeks after Nationals. We did not really know what to think about earning the bid or competing in Globals, and we had never really planned for it. And we did not really focus on it because our sole emphasis was getting our girls to Disney for the first time.

But if we had any chance of making it to Nationals, we had to practice more than we ever had before. We took another two weeks just to improve our routine. To get some extra competition practice, the coaches decided that the squad should compete at the State level competition. In most years, the

Wildcats did not compete at States. This is because the New Jersey State Cheer Competition was not necessary to get to Nationals, so we had never done it before. (Yes, cheer competitions are complicated!)

But this year, it seemed like a good idea for the girls to do their new and improved routine in front of an audience before the big competition a week later. We thought that another day of the pressures of competition and another set of score sheets from the judges would make it better for us. That this could be a great learning experience for us before Regionals. We were so wrong.

This turned out to be a terrible idea because many of our girls also played competitive softball, so we had decided to ask if we could be the very first team to compete that Saturday morning so our softball players could hit the diamond that afternoon. This meant we were at the arena while it was still dark, and the girls were tired. It also meant that the crowds were lighter than they would be later in the day, and there would not be as much energy in the arena for the girls to feed off of.

Even during our warm-ups, we were falling flat, a lot was going wrong, but for some reason, we also did not take any of it too seriously. We tried fixing a few things, but we figured the girls would pull it together like they did in practice and hit their routine once they hit the floor. The coaches said their goodbyes, and the girls went into the tunnel.

When they took to the mat, they were technically okay, but they lacked energy, and they lacked spirit. They were just there. They were not as great as they usually were, and it was getting increasingly obvious throughout their performance. Some of the girls were tired from having been at Six Flags the night before. It all showed.

There were not have any major problems, but we lacked any and all spark that the team normally had. As a result, we scored in the middle of the pack. We were the Central Jersey champions, and we did not show it at States. We did not perform like champions and lost at a competition we did not even need to be at. It was a little disheartening for the team and the coaches, but we still had time to improve.

We still had a week to get the ship right and get the girls focused for Regionals. But we were never able to shake what happened at States, our bad performance stuck with us, and I did not know if the girls would be able to perform their best with this lingering in our minds. We went through the same processes, and even had a pretty good warm-up before taking the floor. We were really good at Regionals, but still not as amazing as we had been at Central Jersey. Would we ever be able to be as great as we were that one time? Only the top two teams would move on to Nationals.

After finishing the routine, we still believed we had a chance at winning and moving on. But when the scores were announced, we came in fourth place. There would be no invitation to Disney for us again that year.

Our girls were absolutely devastated; they had wanted this more than anything. The head coach was down on the floor waiting for score sheets, so it was left to me to speak to a dejected and heartbroken team when I myself was completely devastated. So I did what any good coach needed to do; I told them how incredible they were. I tried motivating them even though I knew we were all upset and it was okay to be, but I did not want them to leave thinking they were not great cheerleaders.

They had worked hard all season, and despite everything, they were the Central Jersey champs, and no one could ever take that from them. I told them that they did well that day, but it just was not meant to be. And we knew we would learn from all of this, and we would be a better team next year.

We dried our tears, gathered our things, and prepared to leave the arena. We said our goodbyes to each other and gave everyone hugs. They may not have won, but they were a team, and they were friends; this team meant a lot to these girls. And with that, another season was over.

Chapter 11

YCADA Globals

"Nobody is gonna hit as hard as life, but it ain't how hard you can hit. It's how hard you can get hit and keep moving forward. It's how much you can take, and keep moving forward. That is how winning is done."

— Rocky Balboa

Our season had ended in disappointment, but we were still a team; we didn't want them to just go their separate ways and lose the connectivity as a team that we had spent so much time developing. In the lead-up to Regionals, we had promised the girls that if they attended all of the practices and gave it their all, we would treat them all to a movie in December. And they lived up to our expectations better than we had even hoped for. So, in mid-December, we all met up at a local theater to see The Grinch.

As we waited for the movie to start, we noticed that the girls were huddled together in circles, with us coaches unsure why. After the movie was over, the girls told us that they wanted to talk to us about something.

They had remembered that back in October we had won a bid to Globals, that new competition that was scheduled for January, and they wanted to know if it was something that we could still do. Honestly, I had not given the bid much thought since the day we earned it; I did not even know what it really meant. But they were right. We had the right to go to Globals if we wanted to.

We did a quick survey of the squad, and it turned out that most of them wanted to give it a try. Luckily, it was taking place in Atlantic City, not too far for us to get to from the other side of New Jersey. Unfortunately, a few of the girls, or rather their parents, decided they did not want to participate, for a variety of different personal reasons. Three of our strongest cheerleaders were done for the season. But the rest of the squad wanted to continue, and so we would.

We decided to bring up two girls from the Junior Pee Wee squad who were with us the year before to add to our team for the Globals competition. Unfortunately, once we made the decision to do this, we did not have much time. We only had a month, including Christmas break, to pull it all together, even more challenging with the changes to the squad. But the girls buckled down, and we practiced three nights a week, getting better and better at the routine every practice. There was a lot to be done, but we worked around the departures and soon were ready to do our routine one final time in front of the judges.

The competition was on MLK weekend at a casino in Atlantic City, and we were to compete on Saturday morning. We were scheduled to head down to Atlantic City the night before to get ready and have a cheer party with the other squads; as we knew the girls would do better if they had some fun before a competition. Tuesday night, a few days before our departure, would be our last practice before heading to the shore.

We planned to have a relaxed and fun final practice. This is what we had been doing for months; for some of the girls who arrived at practice early, we allowed them to work on their tumbling or play on the gym's tumble track, the long trampoline where they could get the extra bounce to work on flips and jumps. Our strongest cheerleader, a base who is the head coach's daughter, was running on the tumble track, doing the same thing she had done dozens of times before. But that day she came down with her foot partly on the track and partly on the frame. She let out a scream and crashed to the ground.

Hearing the shriek of pain, the coaches immediately ran to her, and all the girls started gathering around as well. It turned out she blew out her knee. She spent the rest of the evening in the emergency room with her mom, our head coach, trying to figure out what was wrong. The rest of us were left to pick up the pieces and figure out the next steps.

The girls in the gym were an absolute wreck seeing their teammate and friend in such agony. They all started talking about wanting to quit right then. All motivation had flown out of the room, and none of them wanted to leave a team member behind. They could not go to Globals without their friend. They just could not cheer without her, both emotionally and practically, since she was our strongest base.

I called the girls around and gave them all another pep talk. I told them we did not know what was wrong with our teammate or if she would be able to rejoin the squad that week (though after helping carry her downstairs at the gym into her car, I suspected I knew the answer to that). But I wanted to keep their spirits up; they had to keep going for the team, and for their friend. Giving up was not the right decision. If anything, they should try their best to win for their hurt teammate, and we needed to do our best and finish what we had committed to. We were Wildcats, and we needed to show Globals how strong we were.

But this injury meant that we were a cheerleader down, and short a team member who was very vital to the routine. We spent that evening figuring everything out, trying different combinations of groups, and we quickly changed up some assignments on the mat to fill the newly created hole. We tried to make it as easy as possible for everyone to adjust to the revisions, and we just looked to do a routine we could actually complete just a few days later.

We looked okay that evening but still had more practice to do and more things to work out. While we had initially thought we would have Thursday off, things had changed drastically. We decided we needed one more practice to see if we were even able to do this.

That final practice went surprisingly well. We signed a get-well card for our hurt teammate and showed the head coach all the changes we had made. And then, based on her opinion, made more changes. We did the best we could.

On Friday, we broke most of the girls out of school early and caravanned down to Atlantic City. Of course, I had to be in NYC for a big work meeting that morning, so I ended up rushing home early that afternoon and then driving to Atlantic City by myself. It gave me way too much time alone to think and ruminate about what was going to happen.

That night, our cheerleaders and our coaches attended a cheer "formal" put on by YCADA, which I ended up leaving early, as five members of the squad wanted me to take them to the beach, in mid-January, in New Jersey, in the freezing cold, just so they could take selfies. It was worth it to see them so happy and just enjoying themselves. They had never been so relaxed before a competition.

Later that night, we tried to replicate what we usually did the night before a competition. We threw a curling party in the hotel, we got pizza and soda as we readied ourselves. As we got ready for bed, my daughter tried to convince me to let a friend on the squad sleep with her in our room and that I could go stay with the friend's mom. That was never going to happen, but other than that, everyone was in good spirits.

The morning of the competition was typical for us; it was expectedly chaotic. As always we could not find some cheer shoes and uniform pieces. We decided to all get together for a team and family breakfast in the hotel. The breakfast was an utter disaster; it took way too long, it was way too expensive, and it had everyone on the edge. But if this was the worst that would happen to us, we would be okay.

It was then time to get ready for the competition. We started in the quiet room where the entire squad sat around in a circle, and we all shared our feelings and what we were most grateful for. I had not realized how emotional this was going to get because, by the time the coaches had finished, everyone was crying. I told the girls how proud I was of them, not for being champions but for persevering. Each of them was like a daughter to me, and I would do anything in my power to help them. I could not be prouder of them, no matter how this competition turned out.

We then moved onto the warm-ups, and the girls got to the practice mat to run through the routine. It was awful, worse than anything you can imagine. It may have been the worst that they had ever been before a competition. Typically, we would want more time to walk through things again on the mat, but we just stopped the walk-through this time. There was nothing we could do at that point, and we just had to finish the season no matter what happened.

The Wildcats took to the mat, and the coaches were all in the front row watching, holding our collective breath that it wouldn't be a complete disaster. The music came on, and the girls started. What happened next was something I had definitely not expected. It was unlike anything I had ever seen. They hit everything they needed to. They were near perfect. Each stunt. Each tumble. The pyramid. Everything was as it should be. And the energy and smiles were unlike any other competition. Clearly they had channeled all their anxieties and concerns for their hurt teammate into the routine, and they nailed it.

This was the best that the Wildcats had ever been. I was shocked; all the coaches were shocked. This was not the same team we saw during warm-ups. Something had changed, we didn't know what, but whatever it was, they were terrific. They were perfect. We didn't know how they COULDN'T be champions.

As we were leaving the mat, the announcer called me over to the center of the stage. At most of these competitions, I stuck out like a sore thumb. Not only was I a male coach, but I dressed the part of a cheer coach on steroids. There I was, in a sparkly feather boa, an orange tutu, and an orange fedora with a cheer bow attached to the side. As I talked to the announcer, all I could do was tell the crowd how incredible our girls had been. If only they had known we had lost one of our top athletes just a few days prior and had redone the routine just days before.

The wait for results was far longer than it had been at any previous competition. We were nervous and excited because we knew we had done well. Now we just wanted to see how well we did in the judges' eyes.

When they announced the results, though, we were once again disappointed – we took third place. How could that be? We had the crowd rocking! We had watched the squads that placed ahead of us, and I believed that we were much better than them. Even after deciding to continue our season, we once again ended on a disappointing note. It was disheartening, to say the least.

We collected uniforms from the girls right there in the casino, not knowing when we would get together again. I ended up driving my daughter and two other girls home, as they would all be staying at our house that evening. To my surprise, they were all in good spirits. They knew they had done a great job and knew they had left it all out on the mat. Cheer was a subjective sport, and they were well aware of this. They did not win much better than I did.

A few days later, we received an email from Globals, and it turned out that there had been a tabulation error, and we were actually Runners Up, not third place! We had taken second place!

While we never got the chance to celebrate the second-place finish in front of our families or to get our Globals Runners Up banner from the judges (yes, YCADA, you still owe us that banner!), we could walk away from the season knowing that we were among the top squads in the country.

To this day, I believe that the only reason we did not win was that the squad awarded first place at Globals had just a month earlier been the first-place winner at Nationals. There is no way that the judges could have the Nationals winner lose to a team that hadn't even qualified for Nationals. But then again, I am biased, and I would defend my girls at any time. I am just glad they got the title they deserved and worked so hard for.

Chapter 12

Better Coach for My Cheer Daughters

"You control your destiny. You don't need magic to do it. And there are no magical shortcuts to solve your problems."

— Merida, 'Brave'

The WWP Pee Wee Wildcats had won second place at Globals, a feat WWP had never previously achieved. In my eyes, those thirteen girls, as well as their injured sister, showed the heart, the perseverance, and the showmanship of true winners. Regardless of their final score, they were all champions.

They taught me the definition of teamwork because it was the squad, the girls, not the adults, who decided to accept an invitation to compete at the YCADA Globals cheer competition, deciding to take on two more months of unplanned practice so they could end the season their way, on their terms. And that's exactly what they did.

And they taught me the true meaning of perseverance by rallying after losing one of the leaders of our squad to an awful sports injury just two days before we were to depart for the competition. After drying off our collective tears and agreeing we needed to carry on, we had to significantly rework our routine, asking girls to take on responsibilities they were not ready for. The squad took the mat after only having practiced the new routine for a collective two hours before stepping out on the Globals stage.

But they had managed to do it, and they were terrific; they were better than everyone else. They placed second, but they were the real champions in my eyes.

We had about six months to regroup, and we would need to see what the next season would bring. It was mid-January, and training camp would start again on the first of August. We certainly knew nothing was ever easy; we already knew a few girls would not return to the squad for various reasons. It was always disheartening to lose members of the squad, but we always kept going; it is who we were. We knew we would bring a few girls up from Junior Pee Wee, and we knew we needed to do everything possible to make a dream come true and get our squad to Disney for Nationals at least once in our life. Many of these girls (and coaches) had been cheering together for five or six years, and they had never made it to Disney. This was also going to be the last year of cheer for many of the girls. It was always the big dream for the girls, and so it was my dream too.

But to help fulfill that dream, I realized I, too, needed to improve, and I needed to get better at my coaching. Having entered all of this on a whim, to support Anna, I had known nothing two years prior, and I was still learning on the job. I began as a coach, believing that I would just stand in the back, maybe carrying some mats when needed. I could not have been more wrong. I learned vocabulary and motions, figured out how to stunt and step in to instruct and direct when needed. But I never fully understood the hard work it took to be a coach. I could appreciate that it was not a sideline position; I knew just enough to know that being an effective coach was a significant role that I had yet to fulfill correctly. So in May, I headed to Las Vegas for a YCADA coaches conference. I thought it would be valuable to spend three days learning from the best in the field about being a good coach.

And I was entirely right about this. In just that short time I learned so much about how to coach. They taught me more about how to choreograph and motivate our girls. I even learned how to better understand scoring, which was useful because I often realized my perception of what was good at a competition was far off from the judges'. Overall, I left that conference as a better coach and a better me. I was one of a few men attending the conference.

I was also the only coach from our community who attended. During the first night's happy hour, I was "adopted" by another group of female coaches who tried to convince me to go out with them on the Las Vegas Strip that evening. The next night, I had another coach slip her room key into my pocket, telling me that "what happens in Vegas stays in Vegas."

I do not know if many of the other attending coaches were just not serious about the conference, attending as an excuse to have a Vegas vacation. But that was not why I was there. I was not opposed to having fun, but our ideas of having fun were different. (And my idea of fun is definitely NOT cheating on my wife, which she appreciates as well!) I was here to learn. I passed on both invites and instead focused on the conference sessions. I was there to be a better coach for my daughter and my cheer daughters.

When most people hear that I am a cheer coach, they usually give me bizarre looks and ask even odder questions. Often they ask if I was a cheerleader in high school or college, looking at me quizzically since I physically don't look like I ever had a cheerleader's body. I know that most of the football dads in our community just did not get it. I know that many others were not initially sure what to make of it. But as I looked back on the past six months, on our more than 100 hours of practice and our four competitions this season alone, I was enormously grateful for each and every moment of it.

I was grateful to have a front-row seat to see such incredible student-athletes grow into incredible leaders and young women. I was grateful to be part of a team that could work through all the drama from both competitive sports and being tween girls to become a highly successful unit. I was grateful to work alongside absolutely amazing cheer coaches who give their time, hearts, and souls to help these young women achieve their goals.

As our squad prepared to take the mat for the final time that season, I had urged them to enjoy each other, support each other, help each other, talk to each other, be there for each other, and love each other. With misty eyes, I watched each of my girls walk off the mat after their two-and-a-half-minute routine, knowing they had done their best and ended their season on a note of great pride and success.

When I began my "career" as a cheer coach, I never expected that I would become as invested in and connected to cheerleading and my squad as I have. I may have a football lineman body, but I now know that I have the heart and mindset of a cheerleader. I hope I encouraged and inspired the members of my squad with each practice and gave them the support they needed, as they needed it.

After two seasons, I was proud to be a WWP Wildcat cheerleader and proud to have the privilege to spend time working with incredible women and amazing young women. I wear the label "boy cheer coach" with immense pride. But I knew I needed to be better.

All I had to do now was try to be the coach that all the women (young and old) deserved; they were so talented and deserved that I try my best. My focus in Vegas was not the same as some of the other coaches in attendance. All I was there to do was learn and improve for the team. I needed to be better for my girls.

Section 3

Achieving the Disney Dream

Chapter 13

Pushing Harder

"Sometimes the right path is not the easiest one."

— Grandmother Willow, 'Pocahontas'

Summer rolled around again and the excitement for the new cheer season started to build. It was a new beginning for us to do it all over again, to build on the successes of the previous season but do it even better. The start of the cheer year and training camps was the same as the previous two years. It meant bringing together this group of incredibly talented and enthusiastic girls who were still riding high as runners-up at Globals.

We were all still a little giddy from that win because it came after what had been an absolutely heartbreaking season for us as a team, losing at Regionals and not making it to Nationals. Our performance at Globals gave us hope. We saw that if we believed in ourselves and in each other, magic could happen. It was time to get our act together; if we wanted to get to Nationals and achieve our dream of Disney, we had to learn from past mistakes and previous heartbreak.

It was the same summer drill, practicing, trying to build the pieces of the routine, trying to improve everyone's foundational skills. We spent so much time figuring out how and what we could do better; we wanted to learn as much as possible from the previous season.

The only difference about this summer was that in past years we usually knew who we were competing against; we always knew our competitors because they were from the same local community. This year would be different. The governing organization had gone through some significant consolidation of regions, so we suddenly had more teams in our division, including some that had gone on to place at Disney in the past. In previous years, we at least had an idea about what our competition was like, about their abilities and talents, but now we were in the dark with many teams.

The consolidation was due, in part, to various concerns by parents who thought their girls should not compete as it was too dangerous. There were fewer squads and fewer cheerleaders in New Jersey than in previous years. While understandable, this consolidation of different leagues meant that many of the teams we previously wouldn't have encountered until Eastern Regionals, if even there, would now be competing with us at Central Jersey, our very first level of competition. And these were all fantastic teams.

It meant that it would just be an incredibly difficult process for us to even advance from the first, Central Jersey, level, a level in which we always came out near the top. Usually, we could typically go into Central Jersey believing that we could take second place even on a bad day. But, now our routine would have to be really strong right from the beginning, and even then our chances were lower than usual.

On paper, the path ahead was simple. First and second-place teams at Central Jersey move on to Eastern Regionals. The top two or three teams at Eastern Regionals would move on to Nationals at Disney. In the past, we were confident we could take first or second at Central Jersey against the typical competition. But with the consolidation, this now was not a typical year. The coaches all knew that it would be terribly heartbreaking if we did not even make it past Central Jersey.

This season was different, and it was difficult; they had added in many new teams, but there was one team, the same Hillsborough Dukes who had tried to poach Anna a year prior, that goes to Nationals every year, and they were being injected into our division for the first time. So it meant we had to take a very different approach. If we did not improve and if we were not absolutely perfect at the first competition, it could be over for us. We entered the season knowing that it was possible we would have only one opportunity to compete, and then we could be done. This forced us to really push our girls harder than we had before. But this would not be easy; working this hard is not easy, particularly for a group of tween, many becoming teen, girls in the early stages of puberty. We had a lot of emotions, we had a lot of frustration, and we had issues that came up almost from the start.

These issues were new for the coaches and for the girls to deal with as a team, and they soon started getting the better of us. This was the first time we had any major problems with the girls fighting with each other, and we were dealing with everything from slights and issues in school to concerns of bullying and cyberbullying. It was having a serious effect on our team and our girls.

I hated the fighting not just because we were a team, a family, and it hurt me to watch the girls fight with each other like this, but it was particularly hard for me because my daughter was in the center of one of these issues. At one practice in September, it came to a head right on the mat, where all of a sudden, some of the girls, including my daughter, started getting physical with each other. As coaches, this took us by surprise and we were largely clueless about what to do and how to solve all this drama. It was tearing the team apart.

At this point, we were just trying to hold it all together! There were fights between girls, bullying, and a severe lack of motivation. The problem was not simple, and we had had nineteen girls, all of them eleven to fourteen years old. It had become much harder to coach them and much harder to manage them because they wanted to be on their phones, and they were constantly goofing around and rejecting authority. It was typical teen behavior, but it took a toll on our performance and practices.

There were many times during the season when we had to make it very clear that we could – we would – just stop if they did not want to do this. We did not want to force them to compete, but this was not something we could go into half-heartedly, especially since we were putting in so much time.

And when I say a lot of time, I mean it. They were dedicating the entire second half of the summer to cheerleading practice: again, about two hours a night, four nights a week for the entire month of August. And when September rolled around, the schedule again shifted to three practices a week for two hours each plus a football game on Sunday.

So, we were basically talking about ten hours a week of practice, much of which was going to waste if their hearts were not in it or if they were wasting time fighting or dealing with drama spilling over from school. If these athletes did not want this, then there was no point in spending all this time practicing. When practices went on and the girls regularly were not paying attention, it was shaping up to look like a disaster.

Things were looking so bad that on several occasions, I, typically Mr. Positivity at practice, would have to tell the girls we can just quit the season now. And all of this just made for a hard couple of weeks because the clock was ticking, loudly. We were supposed to be getting ready for Central Jersey, the third week of October. We were supposed to focus and improve, but instead, the girls lacked focus, and nothing came together; I was not sure what would happen at Central Jersey if we continued like this. I worried our streak was coming to an end.

Chapter 14

Getting Ready for Central Jersey

"The very things that hold you down are going to lift you up."

— Timothy Mouse, 'Dumbo'

This season was shaping up to be one of the toughest we had so far, and it had not even started yet; everything was an absolute disaster. No matter how hard we tried, things were just not coming together, and Central Jersey was looming. I loved these girls, and I believed in them. I always have and always will, and I knew they were terrific, but I did not know if we would be good enough by the time we had to compete.

All along, the fighting and lack of focus among the girls led to problems, but it got out of hand when two weeks before the competition, we dropped one of our flyers in practice. It was an accident but one that was a consequence of the girls being distracted constantly. Girls fell all the time, but this fall caused the flyer to dislocate her elbow. It was a terrible moment for all of us, and brought back the pains of the previous season.

We were a squad of 19, but we really did not have many people that could replace her and take over her role. Being a flyer was challenging; not many of the girls were qualified to do what she did, and now we had lost one of our best team members because of our issues as a team. We had to figure out what we were going to do.

During all this chaos, my daughter was having a tough time. She had gotten wrapped up into some of the drama, and her heart was not necessarily in cheer. Besides getting easily frustrated, it was making her question if she even wanted to cheer anymore. She was not sure if she fit in with this team. But she felt like she had to be there because of me. Despite all these things she was feeling, in the practice where the girl dislocated her elbow, Anna pulled me aside and told me that she would step into her friend's role.

It was huge that she decided to step up for the team when she had not been having a great time with them. She was never one to volunteer, but this time she stepped up because no one else did, and we needed a flyer (even though I think Anna was often afraid to fly at this point). She was afraid people would drop her, and she was afraid of getting hurt. (All very reasonable concerns, especially since someone had just been dropped and injured!) She had lost the confidence she previously had, and as the high-profile, most visible position, flyers needed to ooze confidence.

Anna somehow rationalized that she would not get hurt because it was not her original role in the routine. She was just doing it for somebody else, and she could not get hurt because that person already got hurt. It was a convoluted rationale, but at least it got her to volunteer. I was proud of her for stepping up and for wanting the best for the team despite everything that was going on.

Over the course of the next two weeks, we had to figure out how to not only how to coach my daughter to be a flyer again but also get other girls to do it with her who had not done it with her before. But we had to do it, there was no other option, at least in my mind.

Before we knew it, the competition was here, and as we did every season, all the girls hung out together the night before. It was a ritual that we would never miss out on, no matter how bad things got. We got all of the girls together and had the curling party. All the moms were there and were getting the girls ready in their uniforms and setting their hair.

We were also trying to get them ready mentally by loosening them up a bit emotionally before the competition. I knew things had not been great, and so did they, but we did not want them to go into the competition feeling this way. Amazingly, that night it was almost as if a switch had been flipped, and all of a sudden, the girls seemed to finally come together as a team. It was incredible, and it was just what was needed; it took a while, but I was just glad we got there, that we were a family again.

I think there were couple of things that made a difference for the team that week. First, a couple of days before the competition we were able to hit our routine perfectly for the first time. As long as I have been coaching, we have never been a good practice team, so this was big for us, it really helped the team gain confidence in themselves. This was on Thursday evening, and it was the first night that they could do it all correctly. At that point, the girls could see that they could get it done.

At the beginning of the season, the girls made clear they wanted their own text chain; they used it to go back and forth on all sorts of issues both related and unrelated to cheer. They needed a place where they could talk openly and freely to each other about all the issues they had. So although we were worried about the petty drama that was likely to come up in such a forum, we told them that they could have it, as long as a coach could be part of it and monitor it.

I was the lucky coach who was assigned to be on the text chain, which meant, on some nights, I had to monitor hundreds of texts from these girls pinging back and forth. So that night, just before the competition, I sent them all a video that I had recorded, just of me talking and reminding them about how special they were, reminding them how hard they had worked and how, regardless of how they placed the following day, all we could do was ask them to go out and do their best.

I realized that we were having confidence issues, but being able to hit the routine perfectly, backed up with me giving them a pep talk, I think really boosted their confidence. They got over their self-doubt and their issues, and they gained a new perspective, knowing now that they really could make this happen.

They were at that particular age where you do not believe you can do it until you see it happen, and once they nailed the routine perfectly at practice, they had their confidence back. It was not until those final days that they were actually able to do it, and that's when they began to believe in themselves. It took some time, but we were finally where we needed to be as a team. Once they could do the routine, they no longer had an excuse to blame everybody around them for why it was not working. They were all still frustrated with the drama, but now it was coming together and thankfully just in time!

Chapter 15

Competition Time

"Do or do not. There is no 'try.'"

— Yoda

It was finally time for the competition, and for most of the girls on this squad, this was their fifth or sixth year of being here. These competitions were things they had gone through and they knew the drill. So, when we got to the arena, the girls were in good spirits, they were relaxed, and they felt good.

The way these competitions work is that each time we have to go through a very rigorous check-in process. They have to make sure that all of the girls match up with the names listed in their books and make sure that all of the coaches are certified and have been approved by the league. We have to prove that every one of us is who we say we are. It is a long and tedious process, but the girls were in good spirits regardless.

We went through all of that, got to our assigned section to sit down for a while, and then began to wait. At some point, we were told that it was time to go downstairs and into the arena, where we then waited in line for our warm-ups.

We stood there in a long hall in the basement of a cavernous athletic arena, and it is just our team, the girls and the coaches.

There is nothing much to do during the wait because we are all feeling kind of nervous, just hoping our turn would be next. As coaches we are sitting trying to keep things loose, trying to keep things light, and trying to keep the girls talking, smiling, and laughing because they could not have their phones with them. It was on us to entertain them.

Our teammate who dislocated her elbow was still going to be a part of the competition. She could not do most of what we were going to do, but she was a part of our team, and she was going to be on the mat with us. Just as we were going down to do our practice rounds, we were told that even though she already had her arm in a cast and a sling, we had to wrap her entire arm in bubble wrap. So we spent some time trying to find bubble wrap in the basement of the arena and luckily were finally able to wrap her securely enough for the judges.

Like any other athletic event, this was going to be the moment where we would know if this was going to be our day or not. We went through the first step of doing the stretches, followed by the second step where the girls practiced tumbling. And amazingly, all of our girls were hitting their tumbles.

Then we basically had just three minutes on the mat to do one run-through of the entire routine. And this is usually where we as a team would see how we were going to do in the competition. In the past, whenever we had hit our warm-up perfectly, we did not do well in the competition. But whenever something went wrong during the practice, the coaches know the girls were going to be okay.

As we were doing our run-through, one of our stunts fell, but we had to remind ourselves not to remind the girls that a mistake was actually a good thing. And after all, it is just a practice. We had a couple more minutes left, and so we worked on our routine as much as we could.

After all this, we came to the painful moment where we place all of our athletes in the tunnel. And all of the coaches have to leave the girls by themselves. But before we left, I pulled aside a couple of our older girls who I considered team leaders (even though we did not have captains). I reminded them that they needed to keep the girls talking, they need to keep them focused in the tunnel, they need to keep them positive. I was proud of these girls because they readily embraced a leadership role in that moment of time when they were all to themselves without the coaches to help.

The rest of the coaches and I went around the other side of the building, and we waited in our own tunnel. And then, when it was time for them to call our squad out for the competition, we were escorted to the little folding chair area. We were again given stringent instructions about how we cannot get up, and we cannot talk, we cannot yell instructions to the girls; basically, we were not allowed to do anything except clasp hands, hold our breath, and hope that all our hard work would come together.

The four of us coaches were sitting together, holding hands when the girls finally came out. It was amazing! They did the routine better than they had ever done it that entire season. It was nearly flawless, and they looked really, really good. And from practice, we knew there are certain moments within the routine where the girls typically have a problem or where something goes wrong. But at each one of those moments, they hit it. Nothing, and I mean absolutely nothing, was going wrong.

At the end of two and a half minutes, we were done. Without even realizing it I was jumping up and down, screaming and trying to run onto the mat to find my daughter. The girls knew they had done a fantastic job, and they were just so happy. Usually, we try not to let them watch others that they are competing with, so we escorted them off. But they were perfect.

We had nothing to worry about.

We let the girls go around and find their parents, who told them how great they were. Then we had time to kill. The girls had not eaten all day so we escorted them to find nachos, crab fries, and the like. After that it was just a waiting game. Only the first two teams would get to go on to Eastern Regionals.

Finally it was awards time. Our head coach and two of our athletes went to sit down on the floor with representatives from every other team. They announced our division results... and we won second place! We knew the girls had done everything they needed to, but we also knew that the team that joined our league was going to be tough competition. Not surprisingly, Hillsborough took first place. We were second, but I knew we were better. In my eyes, we were again champions.

Regardless of placing first or second, we had been outstanding. We knew that at Eastern Regionals a month later we were going to have to face the same team again, as well as additional teams from other areas. But that just meant we had to be even better, because I knew we were better, and I knew we would prove it to the world.

Chapter 16

Eastern Regionals

"Every miracle takes a little time."

— Fairy Godmother

We had less than a month to get ready for Eastern Regionals, and we were going to go up against the same team that had placed first, as well as other really good teams.

Two weeks after Central Jersey, there was New Jersey State, the competition we had added the year before that had been a disaster. Since it wasn't required, we didn't participate this year. I went by myself to the States just to see what we were up against, just to scout out the competition.

At this point, this had been our fifth year of cheering as a family, my third as a coach, and every year, we went into it saying that we were going to earn a spot at Nationals, that we were going to go to Disney. But most of the time, we never truly believed it. But as I sat there watching the squads that we were going to go up against at Regionals, for the first time, I actually felt like we could do it. These other teams were good, but if everything came together, we could be better.

Before the competition, we had the same drill, we had the curling party we always had, and there was also the matter of how we get the girls to believe in themselves. This time though, we did something different. We had 19 girls and five coaches, so each coach took on three or four girls and wrote a handwritten note to each about why she was so special, how much she meant to us, and how much she meant to the squad. At the curling party, we gave each of the girls their notes, hoping to give them a personal, tangible boost that they could keep with them leading into the next day's competition. It was a great experience for all of us because it didn't just help them believe in themselves, but the coaches really meant everything we wrote as we reflected on each of our athletes.

The next day was the usual competition drill, showing up at the arena and going through security. We went through all our warm-ups; we were not as nervous as perhaps we should have been. We knew we were good, and we knew we were up to the challenge.

And they were. When our girls took the mat, they did an even better job than they had done at Central Jersey! They were phenomenal, and they hit everything they needed to hit; they really could not have been better. There were a couple of wobbles, but nothing huge, nothing that was problematic.

We started getting all the girls off the mat and connecting with the parents. And just then, I was surprised to see my daughter an absolute emotional wreck. When they had Anna up in the air for one of the stunts, she knew that she wobbled a little bit. She was convinced that she had done something terrible and that the wobble would keep the team from getting to Nationals and from going to Disney.

Anna felt like she had let the team down. No one else thought this! I had all of these athletes and their mothers that were looking at me asking, "What's wrong with Anna?" Nobody else had seen the mistake that she was so worried about. To be perfectly honest, I did not even see it. But she knew it had happened. And she felt like she had let the entire team and everyone down; with everything they had gone through this season, she was just enormously upset.

And so she was trying to get herself together, and I pulled her aside, trying to tell her she did nothing wrong. All the other coaches were encouraging her, as were her teammates. Everyone was trying to make her feel better, telling her they had done a great job. We finally got her to a place where she had herself together.

Then came the worst part, waiting for the results. No matter how good we were, that wait was never fun. The wait dragged on for hours. When they finally got to our division, they first announced the second place squad followed by the first place team. We knew who our main competitors were, the team who had beat us at Central Jersey, and another team that I had seen at States. We had watched them both carefully when they did their routines to try and guess how the judges would compare us all.

The team we had lost to at Central Jersey had a major problem in their routine, in fact, we were convinced that their routine was a bit of a disaster. We thought there was no way they could win. So when they announced the second place award went to the team that I saw at States, which we felt had done better than the Central Jersey winner, we started looking at each other, knowing that we were the only other team good enough to be first. We just knew it; we were going to be first place.

But when they announced first place, they announced that it was Hillsborough, the team that beat us at Central Jersey. We were absolutely devastated because it made no sense for them to win; it should have been us.

While the top two teams automatically went to Nationals at Disney, there was also a rule that stated if the team that placed third was within 5 points of the first-place team in total score, that third-place team could get an "atlarge" bid to Nationals. We were sitting there in shock, and the girls were crying because none of us could believe we had lost.

As we were waiting, we were told that we had been awarded third place, and our score was close enough to get that "at-large" bid! Our head coach went to meet with the judges and figure out all the paperwork. As we waited to find out details, coaches from other teams stopped to tell us that we were robbed and that we should not have been in third place. At that point, though there was nothing we could do about the order of the awards, we were trying to explain to them, and understand it ourselves, that yes, we had placed third, but we were still going to Nationals.

This was the dream for all of us; most of our girls had never done it before, and we had never been to Nationals as a team. Trying to juggle all of that and make sense of everything was a lot, but we were going to Nationals even if we felt we were shorted on the score sheets. As the shock wore off, we realized that we were winners, and our dreams were finally coming true.

Chapter 17

Getting to Florida

"Our fate lives within us, you only have to be brave enough to see it."

— Merida, 'Brave'

It is hard to believe that after all the emotional ups and downs of the fall, we were finally on our way to Disney in early December to compete at Nationals. This was particularly surreal for me, because in addition to all the drama with the girls throughout the season, I had gotten sucked into it as well. A little over two months before, Anna had been having some struggles with some of the girls on the team, and it became a far bigger issue than I had initially thought. I personally felt responsible, both for not watching Anna closely enough during practices and for not paying enough attention to the growing situation. As we were trying to sort through the issue in late September, I told the head coach that I would step aside for the good of the team. I had offered to resign as a coach for the Wildcats.

I did not want to be the reason that we did not do well at Central Jersey or at Regionals. I did not want to be the reason the girls did not get to go to Nationals.

Fortunately, my resignation was refused. Coach Chris assured me that the issues were not my fault, and more importantly, she said that while she understood my worries, my leaving the team would cause more issues and hurt more girls than I could imagine. So I trusted her judgment and experience and remained a coach.

For the first part of the season, I had purposely stayed away from Anna and her stunt group, focusing my time on other groups. After this incident, I reversed this and spent most of my time on the mat with Anna. It ended up being really good for her and for me.

We had won an at-large bid at Eastern Regionals and now had a month to improve our routine and get ready for Disney. I dedicated more of my time to our practices than ever before while also spending time trying to raise money to help defray the cost of getting the girls to Disney.

We had several girls on our squad who were on scholarship, and we wanted to provide financial assistance to those girls and their parents to make the trip easier to handle. We also wanted to raise enough funds so that we could help every family a little with the costs.

And the costs added up quickly. Every athlete needed to bring at least one parent with her to Florida. We all needed to rent hotel rooms at Disney for at least three nights. Transportation, food, and incidentals were all added to the tally. As coaches, we felt an obligation to do whatever possible to offset some of the costs. That meant asking those with means to make a financial donation to the squad. We also held a series of raffles and football square pools around Thanksgiving weekend football games. And we even had a local restaurant, Aljons, that was kind enough to offer us 10% of sales for an entire week on purchases by people who mentioned the Wildcats when checking out.

Finally, it was time to go. Anna and I were set to leave for Disney early on Saturday morning. We were on a different plane than all but one of her teammates. Anna needed a little bit of alone time and wanted to ready herself for the week ahead. We were flying out of Philadelphia and decided to stay in the airport hotel the evening prior.

It gave us both the opportunity to relax a little and try to sort everything out in our minds. We did not get a lot of sleep that evening, but we were ready for our 6:30 am flight to Orlando the next morning.

Our flight went off without a hitch, and I had arranged a surprise for Anna and a close friend of hers when we got there. I had booked a stretch limo to take us from the airport to our Disney hotel. On our ride to the hotel, we stopped at the grocery store to stock up for the week ahead. Bags and bags of snacks and cases of Gatorade and water for the girls. Boxes of wine for their moms. We were finally ready for Disney.

Our room was not ready when we arrived, so Anna and I checked our luggage (and snacks and drinks) and headed over to a theme park to meet up with teammates. We spent the day and most of the evening at Disney Studios and then at the Magic Kingdom. It was Anna and a half dozen of her friends and their moms.

We were just regular families having fun, waiting in lines for rides, taking selfies, and running through the parks. I think we all ate our weight in junk food. It had been a while since I saw Anna just being a kid. In fact, she had not even brought her phone with her to the park. She was just enjoying the moment. It's all I wanted for her. All the drama, all the angst, it all slipped away as I watched her having fun.

I am a firm believer that something bad happens onevery trip I take. When Anna and I finally got back to the hotel, we were told our room was ready. We checked in and asked to have our bags brought to our room. For some reason, though, the process lacked Disney efficiency. We waited hours for our luggage. Anna fell asleep long before it finally came. I simply fumed. It was not the smooth start to the trip that I wanted.

Sunday was much like Saturday. It was a day at the Disney parks without thinking of cheer. We met up with some friends at Magic Kingdom. We waited in far too many lines for far too few rides. At dinner time, we headed over to Animal Kingdom to meet up with different friends. There, we were able to enjoy more rides and had a character dinner with Chip and Dale. Anna was petrified of meeting Goofy but generally had a good time.

When we made our way back to the hotel, Jen and Michael were there waiting for us. There had been a lot of back and forth as to whether they were going to join us at all. Jen worried that her knees were too bad to do all the walking the trip would require, and we were reluctant to have Michael miss a week of school when he didn't need to. But some of the other moms convinced Jen that this might be a once-in-a-lifetime opportunity, and she would not want to miss it. So there we were, as one happy family, and I could not have asked for anything more.

Chapter 18

Showtime

"If you can dream it, you can do it."

- Walt Disney

Our son, Michael, was accustomed to one or more of Anna's cheermates being at our house every weekend. Just like at home, at Disney the girls were coming in and out of our room every hour of the day and night. It took him a bit of time to adjust to having two, five, even ten girls in our room at any given time. Some of them were searching for Anna, some were looking for me, and some knew we were the place to go if they were hungry and looking for snacks and drinks. Michael tried his best to ignore them, but obviously, it was hard for him. Cheerleading was definitely not his cup of tea.

Anna and I needed to head over to ESPN Wide World of Sports for cheer practice on Monday morning. Now, we had to set aside the fun and needed to focus on the real reason we were there. As a team, we took a bus from our hotel over to ESPN. Most of the girls were not ready for the sensations, emotions, and all the excitement that followed. It was evident on the bus, but we tried to keep it as light as possible.

Once we reached ESPN, we got a chance to take photos, explore our surroundings, and savor the day, making memories that would last a lifetime. Nonetheless, the primary focus at this point was practice. We were allowed limited time on the mat and wanted to make the most out of it. So we went through practice similarly to how we would prep for competitions back home. Not surprisingly, as was pretty normal for us, the practice was a quasi-disaster. The nerves were kicking in, and we struggled to hit our pyramid.

Nonetheless, we tried our best not to let the girls see our frustration since we wanted them to stay positive for the competition the next day. There was nothing else we could do at that point since there was no additional gym time and therefore no way to practice more! We just had to think positively and try to relax. The afternoon after practice we offered to take the girls to another park, but they didn't want to go. Instead, the majority of the girls asked to stay at the hotel and play in the pool, just relaxing and splashing and laughing. Although I tried to get some work done, it was hard. That evening, we tried to return to our regular normalcy and tried to have one of our curling parties poolside for the girls, where the moms curled hair and the girls relaxed and had a lot of fun. We ordered pizza and drinks to make it a memorable competition eve.

We decided that the girls also needed some entertainment, knowing it would help distract us all. All season, the squad had begged the coaches to include the song Apple Bottom Jeans in their routine. We refused because of the somewhat inappropriate content of the words. But they continued to plead, request, and beg. So for the curling party, the coaches decided to put together a spoof song, using the melody and music of the song but singing about the girls. I was assigned to write the new lyrics, and I agonized over every word.

Since I wrote the lyrics, even though I can't sing at all, I was told to take the lead as soon as we got ready to sing. My fellow coaches backed me up. In my opinion, we brought down the house! It definitely got the girls to connect as a team as they all laughed together at our crazy antics. The girls thought it was the funniest thing they had seen in a long time. All the suffering I had while writing the song seemed worth it.

Finally, competition day arrived. Tuesday morning, we headed back over to ESPN to get ready. The girls were in their uniforms, with their hair in competition curls. I wore my version of the competition outfit: an orange fedora with a cheer bow, black and orange feathered boa, orange heart sunglasses, and that orange tutu that a cheer mom had given me years ago, long before I was a coach. For this special day, I had added a black sequined jacket. We were all set for game day.

After we registered our squad, we walked from building to building to get organized and to warm up for our performance. There were thousands of people walking around but I could sense that I was still one of the few men, particularly in a coaching role. There were some male volunteers and judges, and fathers and brothers had come to see their family members cheer, but male coaches were almost non-existent. I really stood out in my competition attire; it was different and eye-catching. As we walked past

the people, many coaches, competition staff, and parents and relatives stopped me and asked if I could pose for a photo with them. I was a cheer unicorn, and they wanted to capture my uniqueness. My girls thought I was some kind of "cheer rockstar." I ended up taking a lot of selfies with people from all over the United States. I was bemused but it was a fantastic feeling to have before the competition began.

For some people, competing is a tough experience, and for others, it is a motivator, a reason for being. I feel like winning is a drug stronger than anything else. Once you get that first place banner, you will love it so much that you will hate even to come second. The minute you become a champion, you want to work harder to experience that feeling again. Nonetheless, the anxious feelings immediately before the competition are usually always the same for everyone.

This was definitely the case with our girls. As the competition time approached, everyone's heart began to race. We decided to spend some moments in the quiet room to share our feelings. As we had at Globals, we used it to show our collective love for one another. As a team, we were far looser than I would have ever expected. The girls were ready for this moment, all set to showcase what they had practiced all this time.

Their enthusiasm and passion showed during our final walkthrough as well. We had our run-through time on the mat and hit the routine. With that, the coaches decided we were done. There was no reason to keep at it since we were loose, confident, and ready after the walkthrough. Now, it was time for the show that we all had waited for – for days, for months, for years.

When you wait for something you really want, time goes by so slowly. It seemed like forever between when the coaches were seated and when our squad took to the mat. It was probably twenty minutes in total, but it felt like weeks. Finally, the announcer called out "West Windsor Plainsboro Wildcats!" Our girls ran out and took their places. It was showtime!

As they danced and jumped with all the passion and hunger that had been building up for so long, I could not have been more proud. As we watched, we felt that our Wildcats were near perfect. I recalled the time at Globals the year before, and it was almost the same feeling we had experienced then. We all were smiling and full of energy. The girls outdid themselves, hitting everything just like they needed to. The audience was totally in love with them. That was it! We were convinced that we were on our way to win Nationals!

With all the effort and time I had given leading up to that day, and seeing the girls represent their hard work and determination to the world in the best way possible, I had never been prouder of them. After everything they had been through this season, as well as the previous ones, they never quit. They achieved their dream of making it to Disney, and they did us all proud.

It was now time to wait and watch the other teams perform. All our feelings were brimming over, and no one could wait for the results to be announced. We were convinced that the best was yet to come and we would be celebrating that night!

Chapter 19

Results

"Life is a journey to be experienced, not a problem to be solved."

— Winnie the Pooh

As I've previously mentioned, once you have given your best, the wait for the results seems to extend forever. I don't know about the girls, but I was excited. After all the teams had performed and we were waiting for the results, we did a series of team and family photos. I feel photographs are an essential part of life; I had never refrained from them even when I didn't like how I looked in them. I am so glad that I captured those precious moments as we waited for the acknowledgement that our hard work had all paid off. Even now, I look at those photos and the beautiful, fun memories and feelings come flooding back. I even remember the music and smells attached to those moments.

After our photography session, we all headed over for lunch. Then there was nothing to do except to wait. It was a warm day, and we spent a lot of time waiting outside. When you do your best and expect an outstanding result, patience is in short supply. At that moment, we were all feeling the same: restless and impatient. But I was convinced that all that waiting would be worth it.

Soon enough, the results started to be announced. The audience cheered at the top of their lungs as they had all been long anticipating this moment, just like us. Everyone was busy in their own activities until the award time came around. We all gathered together, our hearts racing to hear our names being called in the top three.

I was sure that even if not top three, we would surely make it to the top five in our division. To me, our performance was outstanding, and we had stood out among all the other teams. The judges announced the top three teams, and I was surprised that the Wildcats name wasn't called. I was convinced that we would be in either the fourth or fifth spots.

To my utter disappointment, our names were not called out even then. I was shocked. We were definitely better than those teams! The place was rocking when my girls had hit the floor; it was our year! I was expecting a better result, but in my enthusiasm and emotion I had forgotten how subjective cheer was as a sport, as it relied more on the observer than on independent measures.

At the end of it all, we had secured eighth. Our name never was called for the first, second, or third places, or even the fourth or fifth. It took a while to acknowledge that scoring in the Top 10 at Nationals was pretty darn good, but it was still a disappointment. Maybe I had expected too much; I know I was hoping for a better outcome. It seemed to be far more disappointing to me than it was for the girls on our team. They wished that they had won, but at the end of the day, they were happy. They knew it was an outstanding achievement to make it to Disney and to score as high as we did.

As soon as we got done with the awards session, it was time to figure out what we needed to do next. The girls son the squad were fairly psyched after the results, so we were looking for something fun to finish off the day. As we were figuring it out among ourselves, someone suggested we head over to the other arena to get our official team photo. Yes! Another photo.

I felt like my inner disappointment should not affect the girls' mood and dull the environment. They had worked hard for this day and deserved all the good that it had to offer. So I tried to keep their spirits high and showed them how proud I was. The other arena was full of teams when we got there. Everyone was waiting on line for their turn. After our official team photo, we were asked to wait in another line so the squad could get a picture with Minnie Mouse. Excitedly, we quickly shifted to the other line.

After waiting for quite some time, when it was finally our turn, we were asked to show our paperwork. We were a little taken aback by this since we had no paperwork with us. It seemed that the Minnie Mouse photos were only intended for those squads that took first place in their divisions. Our head coach pleaded with the officials for mercy, explaining we had waited in that long line just for that photo. We asked them to make an exception since we just couldn't tell our girls we waited for nothing and the photo would not be possible. Thankfully, they took pity on us and allowed us to get the photo. Woo hoo! It makes the picture with Minnie Mouse all the more special since the coaches know we weren't supposed to even have it. It was indeed an epic experience and memory.

The event was over, and now it was time to head back home. We packed our bags and got ready to fly home the next morning. While I still felt like we were robbed, as I talked to the girls and their moms after receiving the results, I saw no sign of sadness or disappointment. My girls were true Wonder Women with their liveliness, competitiveness, and vigor. I am sure that they will achieve great things in their lives.

They were happy with the results. They were thankful for the coaches who trained them and the parents who supported them. And as I watched their reactions, I realized they were not wrong. We had accomplished our goal. We made it to Nationals, competed fiercely, and placed well, and we should be proud of those achievements. We made no mistakes or errors and gave our best. Our hard work had paid off, and we were champions where it mattered. I remembered a quote I saw at the cheer coaches convention: *"A coach's success is not measured by the number of wins produced. It is measured by the number of winners produced."* That day, I knew I had helped produce 19 winners.

We had worked, competed strongly, and succeeded, just not to the level that I had hoped. It was still very remarkable. What made it all worthwhile was that we had performed for the sheer pleasure of entertaining people and to make our families, our teammates, and everyone viewing us proud of what we did. My mood started to change. I was more relaxed and happy now.

After coming back home, everyone got busy with their everyday routines. It was time for the holidays and we focused on Christmas. Some girls joined winter sports. At the start of the new year, we ordered team jackets for each of the girls to recognize them for making it to Nationals. We wanted to acknowledge their outstanding achievement and let everyone know what stars they were!

A lot of plans were being made at the start of 2020. We scheduled a big party in the first week of March to award the jackets, spend some time together, and begin to think about the new season. But little did we know what was about to happen in the world. We were totally unaware of what the next few months were about to bring and what a dramatic change we would all face.

Section 4

Cheering in the "New Normal"

Chapter 20

A New Year and COVID-19

"Giving up is for rookies."

— Philoctetes, 'Hercules'

Life rarely turns out as we expect. When we stepped into 2020, no one had any idea what was about to happen. Everything was so normal. People were celebrating the holidays, some were making new year resolutions, and others were making vacation plans. However, fate was about to show us a different side of the world, something we never knew about, something that we now call the new "normal."

A week after our March cheer party, the state of New Jersey closed down, including all the schools, shopping malls, gyms, and training centers. We were ordered by the state to quarantine, and months went by without the girls seeing each other. We were locked in our homes as part of the COVID-19 quarantine. The life we had all taken for granted had disappeared in a week.

When the lockdown began, we had no idea how long things would remain like that. Everyone was trying to cope with the isolation. We hoped that things would return to normal in the summer since many people said the virus would go away in the warm weather. In June, New Jersey's Governor announced the restoration of outdoor youth sports as long as the athletes and coaches abided by specific protocols. Under normal conditions, after the end of one cheer season, we waited until the first week of August to start a new one. But of course, after three months of quarantine, we realized this wasn't a typical year at all.

So, for the second half of June, we held outdoor practices in the park for those athletes who wanted to be a part of it. We made glittery Wildcat facemasks and spent several hours each week outside doing strength training, motions, and cheers, all a carefully-measured six feet apart. It was essential to try and bring some normalcy we all missed to the lives of our girls, particularly for their mental wellbeing. We needed to give them something, even if it was just a little bit of what their life had been like a few months before.

Due to the chaos, fear, and extreme health issues rising all over the world, many of the girls were not able to join us. Some parents just thought it was too risky. So we added virtual training classes on Zoom, making practices available there for girls to join us from their homes.

However, at the start of the summer, the local board that administered WWP Football and Cheer in our town, the umbrella organization that administered our cheer squad, made a big decision. It was clear that schools would not fully reopen that fall, and even then most learning would either be done entirely virtually or in a limited hybrid setting. Some of the lawyers on the board believed that our insurance coverage would not let us hold any sort of football or cheer season or at least wouldn't provide any coverage related to COVID. Ultimately, the board decided to cancel the season for football and cheer. It was indeed a tough decision, and the thought of having no football or cheer in West Windsor-Plainsboro in fall of 2020 was disappointing for all of us.

It was a very tough announcement to share with our girls, particularly since the 2020 season would be the last year for more than half of our squad before they would "age out," moving onto high school and out of Pop Warner. So, as a team, we discussed what we could do, if anything.

Considering all the circumstances, and after extensive conversations with parents, we finally decided to try to compete as a "nonaffiliated" independent squad. We thought the competitions would somehow eventually be able to take place. At some point, things had to start to normalize, wouldn't they? We thought we could virtually compete in several fall competitions and would ultimately have the chance to compete in a physical competition in the winter or spring. I even spoke with my friends at YCADA, the group that managed Globals, to see if we could compete there in February 2021 as a "nonaffiliated" squad. They said we could, and that gave the girls and us coaches a light at the end of the tunnel.

Being non-affiliated meant that we would need to find the funds to pay for gym time and other team needs. When we announced our plans to the team, some of our families opted out for health reasons, while others could not manage the cost, particularly since it had been a difficult year financially for many families. So we decided to practice in the park as long as we could to reduce the costs andpractice in a healthier environment while also saving commuting time.

Nine months into 2020 the gyms finally reopened. After all the attrition for various reasons, we had a very small squad compared to previous years'. We also had one new athlete who had never cheered with the Wildcats and two girls who joined us from Junior Pee Wee. Nonetheless, we were a small squad that had no idea what the next day or week would bring; by now we knew that we could be locked in our homes again with no notice since things in the world continued to be very ambiguous and chaotic.

COVID proved that everything around us is temporary. Things that our lives revolved around had disappeared and we were learning to live without them, but one thing was for sure, the team and the people around us kept us going. The passion and love kept us motivated. We tried to make practice as fun as we could. As coaches, we emphasized providing the girls some normalcy in their week.

On Monday evenings, Wednesday evenings, and Saturday afternoons, we were just the Wildcats practicing. When we finally were driven inside due to colder weather, we were able to find a gym willing to take us, even though we had never practiced there previously. We could not wear our "street shoes" into the gym for fear of dirt and virus. While practicing, we took all the safety protocols to keep ourselves and others safe. We had to record the temperatures of everyone before coming in and use hand sanitizer before and after working on our stunting. Things were not easy, but they seemed worth it, in the larger scheme of things. We were doing the least that we could for our girls. We owed this to them and needed to recapture whatever part of their everyday lives we could.

By the end of October, we got used to the sanitizing routine but had no idea about any upcoming competitions nor had we heard any news about a season that we could compete in. The Central Jersey and Eastern Regionals that we used to participate in were postponed until 2021 since New Jersey was still in near lockdown. We started to search for more competitions and finally found a late 2020 competition in Delaware. Soon after, it also got postponed until 2021.

We heard about another competition, but we would have to travel to North Carolina, which just wasn't an option for most of our families. Soon enough, we realized we could compete at Nationals if needed, although the pandemic had forced it to be moved from Disney to the Orlando convention center. Indeed, there were significant concerns related to that as well. It was already a tough choice for many parents to allow their daughters to practice. There was no way we could convince them to let their girls travel to Florida for a week in the middle of all of this.

As a result, we kept practicing and searching for more local or virtual opportunities. Finally, we found a virtual competition where we would tape our team routine on December 12, 2020. This sounded like an appropriate capstone to our season. We had six weeks to get ready while taking a little time off for Thanksgiving, and then call it a year.

As the pandemic continued to dominate our lives, downheartedness and depression started to set in. Feeling down in the time of canceled activities and social distancing was indeed unavoidable, and most of us began to struggle to be optimistic. But depression is more than just feeling sad or having bad days. Anna started to go through the same. As a teen, she was stuck in a negative mood — feeling low and unable to enjoy anything. A social creature at heart, being isolated at home and even in her limited hybrid school setup was taking the toll on her psyche.

As a family, we had to make a tough decision. Anna was not at all happy during COVID. When we started the year, she was not sure if she wanted to return to cheer. Jen and I convinced her that she should finish out her time with the Wildcats, no matter what the season would be like. It was impossible for her to shift to an all-star squad, even if we could find one that was operating, considering the chaotic situation we all were facing.

When we talked with her about cheering, she didn't want to fly, and she also didn't want to tumble – two things that she had loved the most in previous seasons. She hated going to practice, even though it gave her a chance to see her friends. Anna was suffering badly from the Corona depression that so many teens were struggling with, and it pervaded every part of her life. She once found joy on the cheer mat, but now, she hated every moment of it. I think reminding her of what she was missing in life.

At the end of October, Jen and I decided we would let Anna quit cheer. It was a tough decision for us to make, but it was the right one. Anna's mental health was far more important, and cheer was causing more stress and frustration for her and us. Ultimately, we consulted a therapist and stopped making her go to cheer practice. I loved my daughter and just wanted the best for her.

Nonetheless, I still had a commitment to fulfill. I needed to show Anna and her brother that we must do what we can to fulfill our promises and obligations, no matter what. So even with Anna off the Wildcats team, I remained a coach and continued to practice every week without her. Of course, it made me sad not to have her there with me, but I had made a commitment to all my cheer daughters to be there for them too, and I wasn't going to let them down.

We continued to practice, intending to participate and win the December virtual competition. Our routine was coming along, and our athletes started to rediscover their abilities and click with each other again. We decided to practice virtually the week before and the week of Thanksgiving for health safety reasons. Following Thanksgiving, we would have two final weeks of in-person practice before the competition.

Just when we thought things were coming along well, things took a dramatic turn once again. The New Jersey Governor dropped the hammer and issued a new state directive right after the holiday. As of December 5, all indoor youth and high school sports were canceled at least until January of 2021.

There was no way we could practice. Our athletes couldn't meet in person the week before the competition, and we couldn't actually get into a gym to do our routine for the virtual competition even if we wanted to. So the final month of our season was canceled. It was our unfinished chapter to the story we were working on for months. We needed to break the news to the girls through video conference, knowing that if the situation was so severe that sports were being canceled, we of course could not ask them to come together in the gym for a final practice or two. Therefore, my fourth and final cheer season ended with no competitions, no scorecards, no curling parties, and no fun. It just ended with a video call.

Throughout the four seasons, we experienced jubilation and heartbreak. I love all of "my girls" and am immensely proud and honored to have coached them. Proud not because of our Top 10 finish at Nationals or securing second place at Globals, but because they evolved as amazing young women. For all the lovely memories that we made together over the years and all the fun times. Honored because I had a front-row seat watching an incredible group of athletes move from little girls to teens, helping them as they faced huge challenges and directing them into being stronger cheerleaders and better human beings.

My four seasons as a competition cheer coach gave me a sense of purpose and accomplishment. Of course, I owe so much of that to my girls. I also owe so much to my fellow coaches who allowed me to share a cheer mat with them. Even though things didn't end the way we wanted them to, I couldn't be more happy and proud.

Section 5

Life Lessons

Chapter 21

Manning Up for Cheer

> *"Remember you're the one who can fill the world with sunshine."*
>
> - Snow White

People have different perceptions about the sport of cheer based on what they see on TV or movies or what they simply hear about from people. For me, it was never like that. Our cheer squad was a sports team that welcomed all. Our program was open to all girls (and to boys, should they ever choose), no matter what they look like or their experience or lack of. This was not an all-star squad where one had to come with a certain level of tumbling skills. As Heath Ledger says in the movie '10 Things I Hate About You,' *"Don't let anyone ever make you feel like you don't deserve what you want."* All our athletes were deserving.

In my last season, we had girls who had been a part of the team for eight or nine years and also a young woman who was cheering on the squad for the first time, even though it was her last season of eligibility. To us, it was simple. If a girl was willing to put in the work, show up at practice, keep her spirits high, do all that we asked, and learn the routine, she could be a part of the team.

Certainly, this means a significant time commitment. Anyone who signs up had to show up at practices three to four days a week and also to football games every weekend to cheer. For most of the girls on my squad, the games were their least favorite. They joined the squad for the bonding experience that came through working towards competitions. Being a part of the team was their primary focus and desire. Waving pom-poms on the sidelines during football games every Sunday was not what they wanted, but that was a part of what Pop Warner cheer was all about. It was a necessary evil.

Being a competition cheer squad, it was important to understand our standing as a sport. It was no different than playing soccer or softball or any other athletic competition. In the summers, we did training camp right alongside the football team. Whenever I got a chance, I reminded my girls that they often worked harder and did more than the "boys." There is a saying in cheer that says, *"Some athletes lift weights; we lift athletes."* That was indeed the case. When you see three girls toss another girl 10 or 12 feet in the air and then catch her, there is no doubt that cheer is as much a sport as anything else.

Every season, our athletes went through injuries that needed to be managed. In the lead-up to Disney and our entry into Nationals, my daughter had to step in for another cheerleader who broke her elbow during practice. A month later, my daughter fractured her own clavicle, but she continued to compete through the break and her pain. Anna had committed to her friends, and she needed to see it through. She was no different than a professional football player who would play with taped knees or pain shots to get through the game. She was a true athlete who would compete no matter what and push through the pain to the top.

Whenever I hear people saying that cheer is not a sport, it hurts me to the core. It was particularly true in my last season when some teams tried to get around the restrictions and lockdowns for kids' sports by claiming that cheer wasn't a sport (all so they could continue to collect their fees and payments from families). It is an insult to all the athletes who put time and effort into their practices. It's hard enough that cheer is such a subjective sport, and everything happens within two and a half minutes on the mat during a competition. Months of struggle and hundreds of hours of preparation are displayed in those minutes, yet not everyone understands that.

Teams' reputations frequently influence the scores that judges give them. The hardest part is to explain the scoring to the girls. If they drop an athlete, the entire season can be over because of it, but they can understand the deductions that come from a significant error like that. Their season can even be over if they bobble a stunt, lose a shoe, or step over a line. It is harder to explain how two teams can be technically equal in difficulty and execution, but one team gets scored higher because of vaguer concepts like "showmanship" or "spirit."

In cheerleading, there are no makeup games, no "next week" if they lose. In two and a half minutes, a season can rise and continue or be abruptly ended. That is what I call being daring.

In countless ways, cheer is among the most dangerous of youth sports if you look at the statistics around injuries. Accordingly there is a deep commitment to conditioning and strength training to try and keep those injuries from being severe. We need to remind people of the seriousness and rigor of cheer as a sport. Having the courage to put in the time, effort, and focus on something which is so risky, it is cheerleaders' passion that keeps bringing them to the competition mat. Other athletes should just try to do what our girls do!

This can be difficult for some girls to accept, as some of them joined cheer based on what they thought cheer was, but soon realized it was not what they had assumed. While some all-star teams would go with full makeup, we viewed our competitions as sporting events and did not allow makeup during games or competition. No one sees the US Women's Soccer Team walk on the field in full glam makeup, and neither would our girls. They were athletes first and foremost, and we wanted them to realize this and focus on what was important: their hard work on the mat. They wore the same uniform and did their hair the same way not to look pretty, but to not distract from the athletics of the routine. The judges would judge them on the basis of their potential, spirit, determination, and the hard days we went through during practice rather than looks and sizzle. It may have cost us extra style points over the years, which I am sure it did, but it was an important lesson to impart to our girls. It wasn't about selling sexiness. It was about being the best athletes on the mat that day.

It became harder to convince the girls to come together as a team as they grew older. Problems from school increasingly spilled onto the field, whether because of friends or boys or classes. The coaches had to put in the effort to make them realize that in order to be teammates, they don't have to be best friends. We needed to build a sense of trust in the girls that meant that they were all equal no matter what they did during their routine, and no matter what happened in school or in other settings. It meant we were habitually harder on "coaches' kids" compared to the other team members. They could not blame their parents for being late or forgetting some of their equipment or not making it to practice or a game. We treated them as adult athletes, with the respect and responsibility that comes with that.

As time passed, I started to realize more and more that it was important for my athletes to get constructive reassurance and support from me. It wasn't enough to tell them they were doing a great job. I had to be very specific about what I was cheering on and what they were doing well. Of course, my fellow coaches could, and did, say the same things, but I often felt it meant more to the individual athlete coming from me. Perhaps it was just my imagination, but being the only "boy" in the gym or on the cheer mat seemed to mean something.

It seemed like most girls felt very comfortable talking to me about anything without any "filter," whether it was about cheer or anything else. The athletes on my team texted or called me whenever they had a question. One girl even used to Face Time with me at work whenever she wanted to talk. It all seemed perfectly normal to me since I was ready to do anything for these girls. I wanted to support and build them up so that they got better with each practice. But just as important as building their skills on the mat, I felt I had a responsibility to help build their confidence in life. No matter what help they needed or what support they wanted, I was ready to stand up for them, giving them my all both in and out of practice.

I could engage with the girls in a way unlike their moms or even my fellow coaches. I would let a mom know after practice if her daughter did something that she should be particularly proud of or worried about. I was invested in each of those girls, and their mothers knew it.

I also devoted extensive time to pulling athletes aside to talk to them and encourage their efforts. This might seem a pretty normal thing to many, but its importance to these girls was HUGE. Communication is the key. It was important to know if something was bothering them or if they were excited about something, to always try and make sure they were ok with everything. I always talked to them about the good and the bad and I knew enough to refrain from discussing their personal things in front of the group.

I believe I will be the first and last male cheer coach in my community. When I initially started, I know there were quite a lot of cheer moms (and a few dads) who believed it was extraordinary and incredibly strange that a guy was coaching cheer. They watched me carefully during that first summer to try and figure out what I was doing there and why. Even through that first fall, I still wondered what people thought of me, if I was really as accepted as people said I was. Then, in my second year of coaching, something happened to make me realize that I was truly part of the "family." At a competition, one of my athletes heard someone passing in the arena say something negative about me being a coach (probably colored by the fact that I wore a tutu to competitions). My cheerleader asked me, *"Do you want me to do something about it?"* I deeply appreciated that her first instinct was to stand up for me. Nevertheless, I asked her to just forget about it as I had realized it was all a part of the issues around men in cheer.

In my third year of coaching during a competition, a coach from another squad came up to me and said, *"We once had a dad who wanted to coach for us. We told him NO."* At first, I did not understand how a person can say such a thing to another person, but then I responded with nothing but, *"That's too bad."* My girls made me proud that day and validated my statement; we beat that coach's team that day.

I know that I look like a dad who plays football and ought to be coaching it. But I was a cheerleading coach instead, and I am proud to have it as a central part of my life for four years. This sport defined who I am and what my life means today.

Legend has it that our town was the only one in the nation at the time with a Pop Warner organization that had both a "boy cheer coach" and a "woman football coach." I have deep respect for the avid football mind and passion of the woman who gave up hours of her personal time, after teaching all day in a local school, to bring that passion to the boys in our community. From what I could see, the boys on the football team learn a great deal from Coach Jill. It was great to have her on the coaching team and ultimately as a head coach. She knows football and understands how to teach and motivate kids from her day job as teacher. Our football team is better for having her on the coaching staff, as she could connect to the players in ways that some of the dads simply couldn't.

At the same time, I always felt that my role was more significant in pushing gender boundaries, since it is often (not always!) easier for men to accept a woman knowledgeable about football than for men or women to accept another man spending their time doing choreography or such with female athletes.

I would spend a minimum of 10 hours a week with more than a dozen young women while being the only guy. So, I had to understand how to best make that work and what role I would best play. Ultimately, I spent loads of time spotting stunts and catching girls as they fell. I always used to have hair ties and candy in my coaching bag, and as my athletes got older, I had to add maxi-pads to it as well. I took my job as "cheerleader to the cheerleaders" seriously. I prided myself on being their unofficial mascot. For me, it was all about the team. As they say, *"Teamwork makes the dream work."*

I'm also mindful that, for the most part, I was coaching during the "Me Too" era. I always had to make sure that I was never alone fetching a mat from a gym closet with a single athlete, no matter how well I knew her. I couldn't take the risk. I would often drive girls to and from practice, but I tried never to do so if my daughter wasn't in the car. I made sure to tell the mom beforehand that I could drive their daughter home, but Anna wouldn't be with me. Not once did any mom have any issue. They trusted me.

With all the possible problems a person could think of between middle-aged men and teen girls, I learned pretty quickly that I never needed to worry. For years, girls showed up at my house for a sleepover without their parents even checking in with me. We were happy that families were comfortable enough to just drop their daughters off at our curb, watch them come in the front door – often without even knocking – and drive off, knowing that their child was in safe hands. That was the kind of trust level they had. I saw each girl as my daughter, and my "family" grew every year as new girls joined our team. It was a bit much to deal with 19 teen and tween daughters in a single year, but I cared about them deeply and would do anything to protect them.

One of the athletes on my team was an unbelievably affectionate girl. She used to hug me whenever she came to practice. On more than one occasion, I found myself lightly kissing her forehead, as I would do with Anna. I realized that perhaps that was slightly inappropriate, and so I tried to pull back, but the girl got visibly upset, thinking she had done something wrong. I realized again that she needed that kind of support from me.

In youth cheer, especially below the college or even high school levels, a boy cheerleader is almost as unusual as a boy coach. To be honest, it is a real shame. There were many times where it would have been terrific to have some male bases who were strong enough to do some of the stunts that we wanted. But unfortunately, at least in our area, it was never going to happen. The rare boys we would see at our competitions were tumblers, those who were great at gymnastics and needed an off-season outlet to keep up their skills. Of course, most of them were on all-star teams too, but the peer pressure of doing cheer was just too great for a majority of the boys. They didn't want to get bullied about it. It was one thing not to play football, but *why would a boy cheer? It's a girl thing!* Even if that message didn't come from their friends, it often came from their fathers.

It should not matter if my son asked me to coach his football or baseball team or my daughter asked me to coach her cheer squad. Unfortunately, for most people, it matters a lot. Seeing a guy as a cheer coach makes them pause for a moment in surprise and often suspicion. In the beginning, I am sure many parents speculated why I wanted to do it and sometimes the negative thoughts would start to slip in. I know at least a few people thought I must be up to something or that I was secretely gay. But once they saw and understood the commitment I had to their daughters and their team, not to mention to my daughter and my wife, they finally understood, and I felt I was finally accepted.

If people think that I am the only male cheer coach in Pop Warner, I am afraid they are wrong; having been to competitions and coaching clinics all across the country, I know that I'm not a unicorn after all! But for all of my girls, and for most of the squads we came across at Central Jersey or States or Eastern Regionals, I was the only male coach they encountered. I knew I was unique, and I was not afraid to show it to the other coaches who wore shirts and jeans at the competitions. I proudly attended in an orange tutu, a black and orange feather boa, and an orange fedora with a cheer bow attached to the side. I wore sparkles and sequins. I needed to show my girls I was proud of being their coach, and I was okay with being different, so they should be too!

As other coaches (and families!) asked to take photos with me at competitions, the girls found it entertaining. Strangers knew who their coach was, and they couldn't be prouder. I was showing them it was okay to be themselves and be different.

Embracing who they were was the most important thing and the kindest thing they could do tothemselves, and I wanted my cheer daughters to know that!

I want them and all my cheer family to know that I love them and that they have been a great part of my life.

Chapter 22

The Luckiest Man of Earth

"The best prize that life has to offer is the chance to work hard at work worth doing."

— Teddy Roosevelt

As COVID-19 spread more and more, things got tougher for the sports industry, just like other businesses. By the end of 2020, the New Jersey Governor had announced the end of all indoor youth sports for the year as a preventive measure against rising coronavirus cases. We all had long hoped and made efforts to make our last season memorable, but life had planned things differently.

The announcement of the closure of youth sports meant my cheer coaching career was officially over, and it was time to say goodbye. December 2020 marked my retirement as a cheer coach. I felt such mixed emotions: joy to have made such incredible memories as well as sadness around the way it all ended. Not everything in life turns out as we want, but I am still overwhelmed by the experiences this part of my life gave me. The joy, laughter, smiles, excitement, and all the crazy times make me want to shout to the world, as Lou Gehrig did, that I am the luckiest man on the face of the Earth!

It is rightly said that good memories are most often created without conscious effort. Those are the moments that result from selfless actions and behaviors that give of our time, aptitudes, or gifts without any expectation of reimbursement. I fondly remember when I first joined as a coach, knowing nothing about the sport of cheerleading, much less how to coach it. Despite being a huge fan of the movie 'Bring It On,' I did not know a high V from a broken T, a sponge from a cradle. Having no knowledge of the sport and not even sure if I was up for learning it, I took on the challenge simply because my daughter asked me to.

Sometimes, we have to take risks. We have to grasp an opportunity and give it a shot, and who knows, it might ultimately be one of the best decision of our lives. When I signed up for cheer, I honestly had no idea what I was getting myself into.

I will always cherish the four years that I spent on training, drilling, practicing, laughing, crying, celebrating, and coping with my cheer family. To all the girls who ever interacted with me in this time, I hope you all know how dear you are to me. Each season, we spent hundreds of hours getting ready for competitions. Days of sweat and persistence that in due course would be judged by only two and a half minutes on the competition mat.

I don't know how to put it into words, but to say the least, my work gave me a sense of purpose that I never really had before. It gave joy to my life that I never imagined having. I feel like I really have achieved something special in life that many people do not get a chance to experience. What I am today is significantly shaped by my experiences with my girls and my fellow coaches who allowed me to share a cheer mat with them.

Despite having zero experience, I was welcomed with open arms, hugs, and smiles from day one. No one made me feel like

I was learning or lagging behind in anything. That made me all the more determined to learn all that I could. While I was getting skeptical looks from cheer moms and football-coaching dads, I was doing it for my daughter and her friends. And from the very beginning, I was able to do it because of the support and blessing of my fellow coaches. As Gusteau said in Ratatouille, *"You must not let anyone define your limits because of where you come from. Your only limit is your soul."* My coaching sisters never limited me, they always encouraged me.

"If you want something said, ask a man. If you want something done, ask a woman," Margaret Thatcher once said. In all my years as a coach, I was amazed by just how much these women could get done. During the four years of my cheer coaching career, I came across some incredible women of all ages. I have been awed by the diligence, commitment, and enthusiasm shown by these outstanding young ladies and their mothers. Sometimes they seemed to be incapable of competing, but as soon as they performed, they always proved me wrong. It's a bit of a cliché, but just like Eleanor Roosevelt's observation that a teabag does not demonstrate its strength until it gets in hot water, these women were the same.

Christine, Minda, Robin, and Reenauda will forever be my cheer sisters. These four remarkable women have been and will always be an inspiration to me. Throughout my cheer career, they guided and helped me to become a better version of myself, benefiting both the team and my family. On that muggy August day, no one really knew what they were getting themselves into when they let me join them; I hope my part in their lives has been as positive for them as it has been for me.

Each one of these incredible women sacrifices their time (of which they did not have much) to assist our girls. They were perfect role models for these young women, teaching them all about cheer but also about sportsmanship and life. It was not all about winning the trophy, but about the experiences and learning from the mistakes. These are life lessons, not just cheer lessons. If each one of our athletes aspires to be like these four women when they grow up, the world will be a much better place for it.

In some months during these four years, I spent more time with these women than with my own wife. Without a doubt, I texted more with them than I ever have with my own wife! With each practice and season, I felt more accepted into this cheer family. While I may have been the first "boy cheer coach" our town has ever had, and I'll likely be the last, I never felt like I didn't belong or I wasn't wanted. No one except for me underestimated me or my capabilities!

Four years ago, I never imagined that just a few years later, I would have another kinship, another strong bond, another beautiful family with a lot of young ladies from different backgrounds, races, and ethnicities. Sometimes, I was just simply surprised at how close I got to my cheer daughters. I felt like I had 19 daughters, not just one. It was overwhelming and fun at the same time, but certainly, it's not something I would recommend for everyone. It is hard work. But it is well worth it.

The best part of all was that these girls shared every single aspect of their feelings with me without any guilt or remorse. No one made the other person feel embarrassed of something. If one fell down or felt off for the day, others lifted them up, emotionally and literally. At times, I felt like a positive influence on the lives of these girls; they valued that I had made a commitment to them. Whenever I felt any of the girls were feeling low or discouraged after a practice session, I made sure to hear them out. They could share anything with me because I was always there for them; I was their personal cheerleader who would rejoice, encourage, and clap for them in times of high and low. I smiled when they needed a friendly face and was always present when they needed someone to lean on.

We went through heartbreak and euphoria together in those four seasons. The determination to win unlocked doors of personal excellence with these girls. I feel extremely lucky to have seen them evolve as young women who learned the power of genuine and selfless contribution. I had a front-row seat to watching an unbelievable team grow from little girls to teens, assisting them as they came across the massive challenges and guiding them into stronger, resilient cheerleaders and superior, kinder human beings. I love all of "my girls" and cannot be any prouder of them.

These four seasons will forever be a huge part of my life. I am grateful to have had the chance to serve as a cheer coach. While I am sad that I will never wear my feather boa or tutu to competition again, I am immensely indebted to have had the opportunity. I will forever be a cheer dad, a cheer coach, and a WWP Wildcat cheerleader.

www.ingramcontent.com/pod-product-compliance
Lightning Source LLC
LaVergne TN
LVHW040149080526
838202LV00042B/3084